GEORGE ELIOT: A CENTENARY TRIBUTE

Also by Gordon S. Haight

THE GEORGE ELIOT LETTERS (9 vols) (*editor*)

GEORGE ELIOT: A BIOGRAPHY

GEORGE ELIOT

A Centenary Tribute

Edited by
Gordon S. Haight and
Rosemary T. VanArsdel

Barnes & Noble Books
Totowa, New Jersey

First published in the U.S.A. 1982 by
BARNES & NOBLE BOOKS
81, Adams Drive, Totowa,
New Jersey, 07512
ISBN 0-389-20252-5

Printed in Hong Kong

Library of Congress Cataloging in Publication Data

Main entry under title:

George Eliot, a centenary tribute.

Selected papers from the George Eliot Centennial
Conference, held at the University of Puget Sound, Apr.
10–12, 1980.
    Includes index.
    1. Eliot, George, 1819–1880 – Criticism and
interpretation–Congresses. I. Haight, Gordon Sherman.
II. VanArsdel, Rosemary T.   III. George Eliot Centennial
Conference (1980 : University of Puget Sound)
PR4681.G46. 1982   823'.8   81-19088
ISBN 0-389-20252-5   AACR2

Contents

Preface

During the year 1980 many observances of the centenary of George Eliot's death paid tribute to her life and works. Sponsored by the George Eliot Fellowship of Great Britain, a stone was placed to her memory in Poets' Corner of Westminster Abbey, rectifying a century-old injustice. In his address Professor Haight declared that in her hands 'the novel, too long a trivial pastime, became a compelling moral force, which has established George Eliot firmly at the heart of the Great Tradition with Jane Austen and Henry James'.

Another observance was the George Eliot Centennial Conference held 10–12 April on the campus of the University of Puget Sound, Tacoma, Washington. Scholars gathered there from all over the world to hear a group of twenty-six papers presented in George Eliot's honour. The selection offered in this volume will stand as a lasting memorial to her greatness. Limitation of space prevented the inclusion of papers by Henry Alley, Anthony Bradley, James Caron, Mary Coney, Linda Costic, Colin Henderson, David Leon Higdon, Clinton Machann, Meri-Jane R. Mintz, Victor Neufeldt, Ellin Ringler, William Scheuerle, and J. Don Vann.

In acknowledging the part played by the University of Puget Sound as host of this Conference, the editors wish particularly to note the moneys contributed by the Enrichment Committee of the University, the Endowment Enrichment Fund of the University's Board of Trustees, and the Washington Commission for the Humanities. A Faculty Research Grant helped with the preparation of the manuscript of this volume. The editors wish also to express their gratitude for the extraordinary personal support of University President Philip M. Phibbs and his wife Gwen. And finally they offer warm thanks for the invaluable technical and research assistance rendered throughout the Conference and in the preparation of this manuscript by the Conference Secretary Elizabeth R. Danz.

Gordon S. Haight
Rosemary T. VanArsdel

Notes on the Contributors

IAN ADAM is the author of *George Eliot*, editor of *This Particular Web: Essays on Middlemarch*, and of *Ariel: A Review of International English Literature*. He has published numerous articles on George Eliot and is Professor of English at the University of Calgary, Alberta, Canada.

RUTH apROBERTS, author of *Trollope, Artist and Moralist,* and the chapter 'Trollope' in *Victorian Fiction: A Guide to Research*, has published widely in scholarly journals. She is Professor of English, University of California, Riverside.

MIRIAM H. BERLIN has served as Associate and now Visitor at the Russian Research Center, Harvard University. For many years she was a member of the History Department, Wellesley College, and is now Lecturer for the Radcliffe Seminars Program and the Harvard University Slavic Department. She has been Research Director for the Study Committee on Universities and Human Rights of the American Academy of Arts and Sciences.

ELIZABETH A. DANIELS, a member of the Board of Directors of the Research Society for Victorian Periodicals, is the author of *Jessie White Mario: Risorgimento Revolutionary*, as well as many scholarly articles on Victorian literature. She is Professor of English at Vassar College.

GORDON S. HAIGHT, Emily Sanford Professor Emeritus of English Literature at Yale University, is the editor of *The George Eliot Letters* and author of *George Eliot: A Biography*, which received the James Tait Black prize, the Heinemann award of the Royal Society of Literature, the award of the American Academy and National Institute of Arts and Letters, and the Van Wyck Brooks award. He edited *The Mill on the Floss*, the first volume of The Clarendon Edition of the Novels of George Eliot, of which he is general editor. He is a Fellow of the Royal Society of Literature and a Corresponding Fellow of the British Academy.

ROBERT B. HEILMAN, Professor Emeritus of English at the University of Washington, widely known as a critic and scholar, has published numerous articles and books on Shakespeare, the drama, and the nature of tragedy, including *Tragedy and Melodrama: Versions of Existence* and *The Ways of the World: Comedy and Society*, which won the Christian Gauss Prize of Phi Beta Kappa in 1979. He has edited works by Swift, Conrad, Hardy, and George Eliot, and published articles on Austen, Hardy, Trollope, Waugh, and Welty.

JOHN F. HULCOOP, editor of *The Selected Poems of Phyllis Webb, 1954–65*, has also published *Three Ring Circus Songs*, as well as many articles in scholarly journals. His poetry has appeared in all the major Canadian journals, and he is Professor of English at the University of British Columbia, Vancouver, Canada.

JACOB KORG, Professor of English at the University of Washington, specialises in Victorian and modern literature, and is an authority on the works of George Gissing. He is the author of *George Gissing: A Critical Biography*, and has written on Dickens, Meredith, Browning, Hopkins and other Victorians. His recent book, *Language in Modern Literature*, is a study of twentieth-century experimental writing.

JULIET McMASTER is the author of *Thackeray: The Major Novels, Jane Austen on Love*, and *Trollope's Palliser Novels: Theme and Pattern*, and co-author with Rowland McMaster of *The Novel from Sterne to James*. She is Professor of English at the University of Alberta, and has recently been elected Fellow of the Royal Society of Canada.

IRA BRUCE NADEL, co-editor and contributor to *Victorian Artists and the City* (1980), combines interests in Victorian prose and prose fiction with a special interest in biography of the Victorian period. He is widely published in journals of Victorian studies and is Associate Professor of English at the University of British Columbia, Vancouver, Canada.

FLORENCE SANDLER, a native of New Zealand, is Professor of English at the University of Puget Sound, where she combines interest in seventeenth-century scholarship with Blake and the Victorians. She has contributed to *Achievements of the Left Hand: Essays on the Prose of John Milton* (ed. Lieb and Shawcross) and to *Essential Articles: George Herbert* (ed. Roberts). Her work on Dickens, Vaughan, Fuller, and Blake has appeared in numerous scholarly journals.

ROSEMARY T. VanARSDEL, Professor of English at the University of Puget Sound, is co-editor of *Victorian Periodicals: A Guide to Research* and assistant editor of *The Wellesley Index to Victorian Periodicals, 1824–1900*. Her research on Victorian periodicals has appeared in numerous scholarly journals.

MARTHA S. VOGELER is Professor of English at California State University, Fullerton. She has published articles on Positivism, edited the centenary republication of Frederic Harrison's *Order and Progress*, and is currently preparing a full-scale biography, *Frederic Harrison: the Vocations of a Positivist*.

JOSEPH WIESENFARTH, Professor of English at the University of Wisconsin, Madison, is the author of *Henry James and the Dramatic Analogy*; *The Errand of Form: An Assay of Jane Austen's Art*, *George Eliot's Mythmaking*, and *George Eliot: A Writer's Notebook, 1854–1879*, based on a manuscript owned by the Beinecke Rare Book and Manuscript Library, Yale University.

1 George Eliot's Bastards

GORDON S. HAIGHT

Sweeping the field for information, a biographer inevitably turns up occasional bits of scandal. Lady Colefax, who was a famous collector of gossip, once told me some fascinating anecdotes about George Eliot, which had been going the rounds at the turn of the century. Among them was one I could easily refute: that George Eliot had had a son by John Chapman, who was educated at Edinburgh. This boy, born years before she ever saw Chapman, was Lewes's son Thornton, who spent two years at the High School there. But bastards figure in all but one of George Eliot's books. In 'Amos Barton' Miss Fodge is the mother of the sniffling seven-year-old in the Shepperton workhouse. In *Adam Bede* there is Hetty's child—whether a girl or a boy we never learn. Lawyer Wakem in *The Mill on the Floss* 'had other sons besides Philip, but towards them he held only a chiaroscuro parentage, and provided for them in a grade of life duly beneath his own'. His favourite, who takes over Dorlcote Mill, is well named Jetsome. Harold Transome in *Felix Holt* is the son of Matthew Jermyn, another lawyer, whose own parentage is dubious, untraced before charity school and workhouse. In *Middlemarch* Featherstone's bastard, the frog-faced Joshua Rigg, makes an ill-matched pair with his florid step-father Raffles. Tessa's Lillo and Ninna in *Romola* and, in *Daniel Deronda*, the charming family of Mrs Glasher, whose son Hensleigh inherits the Grandcourt estate, complete the list. The one exception is *Silas Marner*: the child Eppie, whose mother Molly Farren, a barmaid addicted to drink and drugs, Godfrey Cass has most improbably married, is legitimate. But his refusal to acknowledge Eppie in Raveloe makes her practically illegitimate.

George Eliot's acquaintance with bastards is revealed for the first time through the Journal of George Combe,[1] the phrenologist. Born in 1789, the son of an Edinburgh brewer, he was deformed and stunted by tuberculosis in childhood. But his mind was sharp; apprenticed to a lawyer, he was admitted Writer to the Signet at the age of twenty-four. After hearing Spurzheim, the phrenologist, lecture, Combe abandoned the stern Scotch orthodoxy he had been brought up in for the new 'science,' which taught him to believe that the bumps on the skull were a reliable index to character. Phrenology, he thought, held the key to all social and moral problems; one's genetic pattern was determined and could be read by the size of the bumps, which he supposed indicated the development of underlying parts of the brain. Morality was shaped, not by religion, but by what he called the 'Natural Laws in the Constitution of Man'. At forty-five Combe married Cecilia Siddons, daughter of the famous actress, and with her fortune of £15,000 retired from business to be the apostle of phrenology. The rage for this new 'science' was as prevalent as that for psychiatry today. Prison authorities called on Combe for advice on the treatment of criminals. Prince Albert engaged him to examine the heads of the Royal children and recommend proper lines of education for them. As a champion of secular education, Combe led an active life, lecturing in Britain and America and meeting all the radical reformers of the day.[2]

Among these was George Eliot's friend Charles Bray, the son of a wealthy ribbon manufacturer in Coventry. Born in 1811, Charles, after a rebellious period of schooling, was sent to a London merchant to learn the trade, living a lonely life in the warehouse. But he found a friend near by, a highly intelligent medical man, whom he may have consulted professionally, a deeply religious Dissenter, who soon converted Bray from an indifferent Churchman to a serious Calvinist Evangelical. His new religion, he wrote in his *Autobiography*,[3] enabled him 'to break away from bad habits and to withstand temptation'. So confident was he of his faith that after returning to Coventry in 1830 he undertook to convert the Unitarian minister, a learned man, who quickly showed him that some of the texts he most relied upon were mistranslations (Bray, p. 11). Bray then began a thorough study of the Bible, which ended before long in his loss of all belief in Christianity.

He fell back upon a crude postulate that 'the laws of mind were equally fixed or determined with those of matter, . . . that *everything* acted necessarily in accordance with its own nature, and that there was no freedom of choice beyond this' (Bray, p. 17).

Phrenology, which he came upon by chance in Combe's books, seemed a revelation of the 'machinery' by which 'the Natural Laws of Mind' worked. Wildly excited, he went to London to have a cast made so that he could examine the skull of the man he knew best, and he purchased 100 other casts showing phrenological 'organs' large or small (Bray, p. 22). His father's death in 1835 left Bray in control of a lucrative ribbon-weaving business with a large income he could use for improving society. He established a secular Infant School, a Working Man's Club, a Co-operative Store, a Provident Dispensary, and supported every reform. In 1836 he married Caroline Hennell, a well-educated young lady from an earnest Unitarian family, and soon settled down in a lovely house called Rosehill overlooking Coventry. During their wedding tour Bray's attempts to explain his heretical religious views had only succeeded in making Cara very uncomfortable (Bray, p. 48). In distress she appealed to her brother Charles Hennell, whose careful survey of the evidence was set forth in his *Inquiry concerning the Origin of Christianity* (1838, 2nd edn. 1841). Moderate and even reverent in tone, his study forced Hennell to conclude that Christianity was not based on revelation, but was simply like other natural human histories, and its miracles merely myths (Bray, p. 49).

Marian Evans had read Hennell's book before she met Bray. His sister, who lived next door, took her to call, hoping that the Evangelicalism for which she had been conspicuous in her school-days might correct Charles's heterodoxy (Bray, pp. 76–7). He discovered at once that Marian's mind was already turned along the same path as his, and she was soon an intimate at Rosehill. He took her to London and had a cast made of her head. Whatever we may think of phrenology, his description, written fifty years later, is interesting as that of one who knew her well:

> The Intellect greatly predominates; . . . In the Feelings, the Animal and Moral regions are about equal, the moral being quite sufficient to keep the animal in order and in due subservience, but would not be spontaneously active. The social feelings were very active, particularly the adhesiveness. She was of a most affectionate disposition, always requiring some one to lean upon, preferring what has hitherto been considered the stronger sex to the other and more impressible. She was not fitted to stand alone (Bray, pp. 74–5).

Charles Hennell's wife, who had begun to translate Strauss's *Das Leben Jesu*, was happy to turn it over to Marian after the first few chapters. Published in three volumes in 1846, *The Life of Jesus* had an incalculable influence on English religious thought.[4]

Combe describes his first meeting with the Brays and Marian Evans in his Journal, 29 August 1851:

> We travelled from Liverpool to Coventry by rail and found Mr. Charles Bray waiting for us at the station, and went with him on a visit to Rosehill, close to the Town. He introduced us to his wife and her sister, [Sara] . . . and to Miss Evans, the daughter of a farmer. The whole party are superior and interesting persons. Mr. Bray is a Ribbon manufacturer about 40; a Phrenologist and a convert to the Natural Laws, with an excellent intellect. . . . He is proprietor of the Coventry Herald, which he uses as the organ of the new philosophy and its applications, so far as public opinion will allow him to go.
>
> Miss Evans is the most extraordinary person of the party. She translated Strauss's work 'Das Leben Jesu' from the German, including the Hebrew, Greek, and Latin quotations in it, without assistance; and it is said to be admirably executed. She has a very large brain, the anterior lobe is remarkable for its length, breadth, and height; the coronal region is large, the front rather predominating. . . and the portion behind the ear is rather small in the regions of Comb[ativeness], Amat[iveness], and Philopro[genitiveness]. . . . She is rather tall, near 40 apparently,[5] pale and in delicate health. She is an excellent musician. . . . We had a great deal of conversation on religion, political economy, and political events, and altogether, with the exception perhaps of Lucretia Mott,[6] she appeared to me the ablest woman whom I have seen, and in many respects she excells Lucretia. She is extremely feminine and gentle; and the great strength of her intellect combined with this quality renders her very interesting.

Three weeks later the Combes stopped again at Rosehill on their way back to Edinburgh. In his Journal 18 September 1851 Combe wrote:

> Mr. Bray shewed me a cast of his head. He has an enormous cerebellum, large lungs, and strong limbs. He is far from being

fond of motion: He eats largely, takes little exercise, and is afflicted by the excessive activity of the cerebellum.

This is the base of the brain, where the animal qualities were thought to reside. In his Journal at this point Combe lapses into shorthand. For fourteen years I appealed to every expert I could find for help in reading these tantalising seven lines of shorthand. In 1977 an article in the *TLS* by Eric Sams, a noted English cryptanalyst, and Julian Moore,[7] impelled me to send them to Mr Sams, and he eventually deciphered them. I am most grateful to Mr Sams for his help, and to Mr James Ritchie, Keeper of Manuscripts at the National Library of Scotland, for permission to reproduce them. The passage reads:

> At twelve years of age he was seduced by his father's Cook and indulged extensively in illicit intercourse with women. He abstained from 18 to 22 but suffered in health. He married and his wife has no children. He consoled himself with another woman by whom he had a daughter. He adopted his child with his wife's consent and she now lives with him. He still keeps the mother of the child and has another by her. I strongly objected to his being cooped up and recommended to him to lower his diet and increase his exercise and by every means lessen the vigor of his amativeness and be faithful to his wife.

The entry then continues in longhand:

> He has large moral organs, with large Destructiveness. Cautiousness is moderate and Concentrativeness deficient. Self Est[eem] and Firmness are large. His family have died of apoplexy at 56 and he says he will die then also. He is in a fair way of realising his prophecy. [He died at 73.]

In transcribing the passage Mr Sams noted that the word *Cook* is written in longhand, presumably because the equivalent is unclear.

It is easy to imagine how Bray in exhibiting his cast to Combe would have confirmed the prominence of its Amativeness with an account of his sex life from the age of twelve. The period of abstinence corresponds exactly with that of his conversion to Evangelicalism, and the 'bad habits' from which he broke away are clearly defined. Though local legend dimly held him to be something of a 'village Casanova',[8] the fact of his mistress and children is quite new.

The earliest mention of a child at Rosehill occurs in May 1845 in a letter from Marian Evans to the Brays, who were at Hastings while their house was being cleaned:

> I had a most gracious reception this morning from Baby, and carried her to my great fatigue to pay our respects to the Cow. The Baby is quite well and not at all triste on account of the absence of Papa and Mamma, whom she invokes very lustily and shows no dismay that they do not come when she does call for them. Hannah desires me to send word that the Cow has not calved and that Mr. and Miss Bray spent Sunday at Rosehill, to Baby's great delight. The young lady's smiles were abundant this morning, interspersed however with frowns which I am afraid she is taught to think as amusing as the smiles. To me they are anything but interesting (*Letters*, I, 194).

In editing this letter thirty years ago I was puzzled by the curiously remote tone of Marian's report to the mother of an infant still in arms. Never called anything but Baby, she must have been born in 1844 or early in 1845. Though Mrs Bray's Diary[9] notes such events as the birth of the Princess Royal and the christening of the Prince of Wales, it has no mention of Baby's birth; nor would her appointments during the year have left time for such an event. The only allusion to Baby is a laconic sentence on 27 June 1845: 'Took our child back to Hampton Station'—presumably Hampton-in-Arden, about nine miles west of Coventry, halfway to Birmingham. Apparently, after two months' trial, Baby wouldn't do.

A year later on 10 June 1846 Mrs Bray wrote even more laconically: 'Brought home Elinor'. This was Bray's second daughter. Like Baby she could have been no more than a few months old; the census return for Rosehill in March 1851 lists her as 'Ellenor Mary, adopted daughter, aged 5, scholar, born at Birmingham'.[10] On Christmas Day the Brays brought her to tea with Marian in Foleshill, and she is mentioned occasionally in the correspondence thereafter. Marian wrote one charming letter to her in 1851 when she was six, thanking her for 'the nice little bag which you and Mamma sent me', signing it 'Your affectionate Auntie Pollian' (*Letters*, I, 347–8). At ten Nelly was 'a tall young lady' whom Aunt Sara Hennell is teaching to play the piano (*Letters*, II, 265). But as she grew up, Nelly's health became frail. Despite sea air and anxious watching, she fell into a decline, and after a long illness died of pulmonary consumption on 1 March 1865 (*Letters*, IV, 179). She was nineteen. 'Surely, dear Sara,' Marian wrote, 'to both you and Cara there must be a sense of having tried to the utmost to give value to that young life which was brought so close to you' (*Letters*, IV, 180). The complaisance with which Mrs Bray accepted her husband's bastards is remarkable. No word of resentment from her has ever been found. During Nelly's long illness Cara looked after her as tenderly as if she were her own, and her death was a genuine grief. Marian wrote to Cara: 'There is no such thing as consolation when we have made the lot of another our own as you did Nelly's. The anguish must be borne...' (*Letters*, IV, 183).

From the beginning Marian could not have been ignorant of the paternity of Bray's children. On her long walks with the 'leaky-minded fool', as Bray calls himself, after Mr Brooke in *Middlemarch* (Bray, p. 47), he probably discussed quite openly with her his way of life under the Natural Laws. How much did her knowledge of it contribute to her understanding of human passions? The tolerance and sympathy with which she treats bastards is unusual in Victorian fiction; we find in her novels none of the hypocritical reprobation that so often condemns Dickens's adulterers to distant exile or death. Compare Mrs Dombey or Lady Dedlock with Mrs Transome. This is not the time to examine each of George Eliot's bastards or to seek their originals about Coventry. Eppie Cass and Nelly Bray are both adopted by weavers—but let us leave these tangled webs to the psychobiographers.

After their first meeting Combe's admiration for Marian Evans increased during the three years while she was editing the *Westminster Review*. They corresponded frequently about articles, and she gave much time to cutting and revising his pamphlet on criminal legislation. In October 1852 she visited the Combes in Edinburgh for ten days. Though they urged her warmly to come again in 1853 and to spend the summer of 1854 with them in Switzerland, she declined all further invitations—and went instead to Germany with George Henry Lewes. When the rumour of this scandal reached Edinburgh, Mrs Combe wrote to Cara Bray for confirmation. Marian's plan to live with Lewes had been confided only to John Chapman, who forwarded her letters, and to Bray, who may have advanced funds for her journey. Cara and Sara Hennell, who had not not been told, were deeply offended. But Cara rallied loyally to Marian's defence:

> We have not heard of anything dreadful happening to Miss Evans [she replied to Mrs Combe], and therefore are quite at a loss to know what has 'astounded' your friend. She wrote to us from Weimar a few weeks ago in high health and happiness. . . . I feel quite sure we should have heard if any mishap had be-fallen her (*Letters,* viii, 119).

Not satisfied, Mr Combe wrote to inquire of Bray, whose reply was no less disingenuous. After recounting the breakup of Lewes's marriage, Bray added:

> His health required that he should travel. . . . Miss Evans has long been wanting to go abroad and Mr. Lewes offered to in-troduce her to friends of his in Germany and leave her there for 12 months, which is what she wished. This is all I know and all I believe and I do not see anything very serious to disapprove in it — at least I *did* not. I see now all that may and will be said about their going together and I think it would have been much more prudent to have others of the party. I can see how necessary it was for Lewes to travel and that he should have a friend with him and that Mrs. Lewes, with her family, could not go, but I fear it was asking too much on Miss Evans part, if she sets any store by public opinion or indeed cares for that of many of her friends. She is just the person however to disregard gossip if a friend wanted her *aid* or I think even if she could go abroad (*Letters,* viii, 122–3).

Still not satisfied, Combe persisted, and Bray answered with quotations from Marian's letters to him. A passage from one of them is of particular interest because the manuscript of it has never been found:

> She says 'I mean this letter for you alone and I beg that you will not *quote* me either in my justification or otherwise. No

one has any right to interfere with my conduct — no one is
responsible for me; and I beg that you will free yourself from
annoyance and enquiries by stating that I am quite too old
< enough > for you to be supposed in any way answerable for
me. So far as my friends or acquaintances are < concerned >
inclined to occupy themselves with my affairs, I am grateful to
them and sorry that they should have pain on my account, but I
cannot think that their digestion will be much hindered by anything that befals a person about whom they troubled themselves very little while she lived in privacy and loneliness'
(*Letters*, vɪɪɪ, 128).

This was very hard for Combe, who felt that he had troubled
himself a good deal about Miss Evans. He wrote again to Bray:

We are deeply mortified and distressed; and I should like to
know whether there is insanity in Miss Evans's family; for her
conduct, with *her* brain, seems to me like < insanity > morbid
mental aberration.

I have no right to dictate to you, but I esteem you too much
not to state frankly to you my convictions.... 'The greatest
happiness of the greatest number' principle appears to me to
require that the obligations of married life should be honoura-
bly fulfilled; and an educated woman who, in the face of the
world, volunteers to live as a wife, with a man who already has
a living wife and children, appears to me to pursue a course
and to set an example calculated only to degrade herself and
her sex, if she be sane. — If you receive her into your family
circle, while present appearances are unexplained, pray consider whether you will do justice to your own female domestic
circle, and how other ladies may feel about going into a circle
which makes no distinction between those who act thus, and
those who preserve their honour unspotted?... I think that
Mr. Lewes was perfectly justified in leaving his own wife, but
not in making Miss Evans his mistress (*Letters*, vɪɪɪ, 129–30).

In his Journal Combe reread his original account of Miss Evans
three years before. In the margin of his description of her Amativeness as 'rather small', he now added in pencil: 'This was written from eye-observation. She has gone off as mistress of Mr.
Lewes, a married man with 6 children. July 1854'. It was hard for

Combe to face the fact that 'the ablest woman whom I have seen' was living with a man who had long ridiculed and derided the claims of phrenology—doubly bitter because it forced him to admit that he had grossly misread her character. For him there were limits beyond which the Natural Laws did not apply.

NOTES

1   National Library of Scotland.
2   Charles Gibbon, *The Life of George Combe*, 2 vols (London: Macmillan, 1878); *The Dictionary of National Biography*.
3   Charles Bray, *Phases of Opinion and Experience during a Long Life: An Autobiography* (London: [1885]), p. 9.
4   *The George Eliot Letters*, ed. G. S. Haight, 9 vols (New Haven: Yale University Press, 1954–78), i, 172–218.
5   She was 31.
6   Lucretia Coffin Mott (1793–1880), American women's rights and anti-slavery reformer.
7   Eric Sams and Julian Moore, 'Cryptanalysis and Historical Research', *Times Literary Supplement*, 4 March 1977, p. 253.
8   Ernest Simpson, Librarian of the Coventry City Libraries, to G. S. Haight, 15 June 1951.
9   Mrs Bray's Diary is found on pp. 190–[203] of her Commonplace Book in the Coventry City Libraries.
10 Public Record Office, H.O. 107.

2 George Eliot's Language of the Sense

JULIET McMASTER

I will begin, not with George Eliot herself, but with that more notoriously licentious writer, Hardy. When Angel Clare returns to Talbothays dairy, hot with his accomplished purpose of telling his father he intends to marry the milkmaid, he encounters Tess still warm and somnolent from her summer afternoon's nap. The passage is heavily sensual:

> She had not heard him enter, and hardly realized his presence there. She was yawning, and he saw the red interior of her mouth as if it had been a snake's. She had stretched one arm so high above her coiled-up cable of hair that he could see its satin delicacy above the sunburn; her face was flushed with sleep, and her eyelids hung heavy over her pupils. The brimfulness of her nature breathed from her. It was a moment when a woman's soul is more incarnate than at any other time; when the most spiritual beauty bespeaks itself flesh; and sex takes the outside place in the presentation (*Tess of the d'Urbervilles*, ch. 27).

Hardy has been very skilful in evoking the intense physicality of his heroine, and his hero's excitement as he glimpses the secret parts of her body and is aroused by her warm responsive somnolence. Hardy has made it his business to delineate the beauty that 'bespeaks itself flesh'. George Eliot, we know, has often presented spiritual beauties — Milly Barton, Dinah, Dorothea, Daniel — and beauties not so spiritual, like the Countess Czerlaski, Tito, and Rosamond — but she has not perhaps had quite Hardy's reputation for considering her characters as flesh. She is an acknow-

11

ledged master in depicting the life of the mind and spirit; but I would like to consider her powers in presenting the life of the body.

Once when I was teaching *Adam Bede* to a class of undergraduates, a student asked, 'But where did the baby come from?' Not that my students in general are inclined to believe that babies are brought by the storks; but they had not understood the language, very clear to a Victorian, by which George Eliot conveys the facts of Hetty's seduction and pregnancy: the pink neckerchief that Arthur hides in the hermitage, which immediately conveys that she has been alone and undressing with Arthur, and that he means to conceal the fact; the change in her that Adam observed, and 'interpreted as the growth of womanly tenderness and seriousness' (27: 338);[1] the unspecified 'dread' that we hear of as Hetty becomes aware she must be pregnant; her expanding waistline which is noted as 'a more luxuriant womanliness about Hetty' (34: 405), and so on. To the reader versed in this language there is no mystery. In fact to some contemporary reviewers George Eliot had been explicit to an embarrassing degree. One offended reviewer complained,

> We seem to be threatened with a literature of pregnancy.... Hetty's feelings and changes are indicated with a punctual sequence that makes the account of her misfortunes read like the rough notes of a man-midwife's conversation with a bride. This is intolerable. Let us copy the old masters of the art, who, if they gave us a baby, gave it us all at once. A decent author and a decent public may surely take the premonitory symptoms for granted.[2]

The Victorian ear was evidently more finely tuned than a modern student's to a language that is allusive and indirect on sexual matters. To the satiated senses of the modern reader, trained on D.H. Lawrence and Henry Miller, George Eliot is perhaps rather stodgy reading. But to her own audience she was often quite shamelessly licentious. A critic of 1867 spoke in alarmed tones of the 'vein of perilous voluptuousness running through her works'.[3] Of course I think the Victorians were quite right. And it is one of the aims of this essay to bring back the voluptuous George Eliot.

Let us consider her first as a sensuous writer. Among the Victorian novelists, Dickens springs to mind as the most sensuous.

Dickens is ebulliently, exuberantly sensuous, and his novels are crowded with vivid sensuous images—with obese curves, dominant voices, savoury pork pies. But the plenitude seems almost a side-effect of his immense energy, and he is always rushing on to something else. Thackeray can be marvellously specific about the things that surround his characters, but his concern is with price, date, quality of manufacture and fashion rather than with sensuous value for its own sake. Trollope's novels, for all their detail about mental processes and human negotiations, are relatively bare of intensely perceived sights, sounds, and smells. But George Eliot made it her business to be full and explicit about sensuous experience. She was a specialist, even able to envisage a state of physical sensitivity so acute that 'it would be like hearing the grass grow and the squirrel's heart beat, and we should die of that roar which lies on the other side of silence' (*M*, 20: 144). That memorable passage in *Middlemarch* evokes a picture of some sensitive Gulliver in Brobdingnag, overwhelmed by the monstrous sensory data that assault his body.

Morever, she makes sensory experience signify more than itself. The degree and quality of her characters' sensory perceptions frequently becomes a means of characterisation. She wrote, in Wordsworth's phrase, in 'the language of the sense', and her language is rich in association and metonymic suggestion.

One recurring feature of her sensory imagery is its tendency to move from the merely sensuous, the neutral registering of external data by the sensory organs, to the sensual, the pleasurable indulgence of those organs. A signal of this movement is the mingling of different sense images: as a sight becomes mingled with a sound, for instance, we are to infer a generalised bodily satisfaction that often approximates sexual pleasure. Dorothea's response to the jewels is strongly sensual, as the visual pleasure seems to overflow from one sense to another. The colours 'penetrate' her, 'like scent', and she looks forward to '[feeding] her eye at these little fountains of pure colour' (*M*, 1: 10).

To start with visual perception. It would be labouring the obvious to demonstrate George Eliot's power to portray faces, landscapes, effects of light and shade. My particular interest is in those moments of intense visual experience that slide towards the sensual and the sexual. These occur predictably in the exchange of looks between lovers. Here of course George Eliot inherits a long tradition: love, say Shakespeare and many others, is first learned in a lady's eye. But she takes the proposition over and makes it her own, dwelling on the complicity involved in the exchange of looks, the rhythm in glance and glance returned, the physical need for the satisfaction of a mutual gaze. The progress of Arthur's affair with Hetty is measured by activity of their eyes: 'Hetty lifted her long dewy lashes, and met the eyes that were bent towards her with a sweet, timid, beseeching look. What a space of time those three moments were, while their eyes met and his arms touched her!' (12: 177). Later they kiss, and then they look again, 'not quite as they had looked before, for in their eyes was the memory of a kiss' (13: 183). With such specificity about the union of eyes, who needs to be told much about the subsequent union of the rest of the bodies? The synecdoche will serve.

It is in *The Mill on the Floss* that George Eliot most fully expresses a sexual relation by giving us the history of looks. Stephen's longing for a look from Maggie becomes an appetite, 'a monomania', and for him the sight comprehends within it the other senses too. In Keats's phrase, he wants to 'feed deep, deep upon her peerless eyes'. His song is Ben Jonson's 'Drink to me only with thine eyes', which powerfully combines imagery of taste, sight, and smell. Maggie responds, also aware that the exchange of looks is more than a merely visual experience: 'she was conscious of having been looked at a great deal in rather a furtive manner from beneath a pair of well-marked horizontal eyebrows, with a glance that seemed somehow to have caught the vibratory influence of the voice' (III, 3: 494). She too becomes addicted to the intense exchange of long looks, and the narrator dwells on the mutuality of this experience they share, in which both must participate, as in a kiss or in the sexual act. 'That mutual glance' is 'delicious to both' (III, 7: 535). Though the Freudian critic David Smith finds that George Eliot 'resorts to vintage Victorian circumlocutions' in the portrayal of Stephen's strong sexuality,[4] the critic for the *Saturday Review* of 1860 was inclined to complain that George Eliot and other women novelists, like George Sand and Charlotte Brontë, 'linger on the description of the physical sensations that accompany the meeting of hearts in love.... We are not sure that it is quite consistent with female delicacy to lay such stress on the bodily feelings of the other sex'.[5] Without going along with its strictures about female delicacy, I'm inclined to agree with the earlier critic in finding the sexual magnetism in the Maggie–Stephen relation quite sufficiently rendered.

'The vibratory influence of the voice' is another of George Eliot's sensuous concerns. Her characters finely register both the timbre of the speaking voice and the emotive power of music. It is characteristic of Mr Casaubon's low-pulsed physical being that he dislikes music, objecting to have his ears 'teased with measured noises' (*M*, 7: 48). And on the other hand the more virile males are characterised by their voices. Stephen has a 'fine bass voice' (*MF*, iii, 3: 494), Adam is a baritone, and Arthur Donnithorne, the seducer, sings Macheath's song about the soothing powers of woman in a tenor. Music is the food of love in George Eliot's novels. Miss Arrowpoint and Klesmer fall in love over the piano, and Daniel Deronda and Mirah first respond to each other through a melody (*DD*, 17: 227). Maggie is helplessly subject to the power of music, which produces a state of 'emotion that seemed to make her both strong and weak, strong for all enjoyment, weak for all resistance'. Her ears are beset on the one hand by Philip's plaintive 'I love thee still', and on the other by Stephen's more decisive 'Let us take the road', another of Macheath's songs (iii, 7: 532–3).

I think the tactual is George Eliot's strongest suit among the senses. She can forcefully imagine, for instance, the special importance of touch to the blind and the short-sighted, like old Bardo and Silas Marner. The blind scholar asks the beautiful young Tito to allow him to feel him, and 'passed his hand again and again over the long curls and grasped them a little, as if their spiral resistance made his inward vision clearer' (*R*, 6: 109). There is a marvellous specificity about that 'spiral resistance' of Tito's supple curls. The touch of hair forms a climactic moment in *Silas Marner*, when Silas, the life-long clinger, dimly sees the glow of the baby's hair in the firelight and thinks it is his gold come back to him:

> He felt his heart begin to beat violently, and for a few moments he was unable to stretch out his hand and grasp the restored treasure. . . . He leaned forward at last, and stretched forth his hand; but instead of hard coin with the familiar resisting outline, his fingers encountered soft warm curls (*SM*, 12: 167).

Silas in fact is characterised by his need to touch. He loves the brown earthenware pot, with 'the impress of its handle on his palm', and his love affair with his gold begins with feeling it. 'The weaver's hand had known the touch of hard-won money even before the palm had grown to its full breadth', we hear (2: 65). This love, like others, comprehends the other senses. In Silas's austere and celibate life there is nevertheless, on its own scale, something like the complex physical indulgence of an orgy, including even the image of procreation:

> At night came his revelry: at night he closed his shutters, and made fast his doors, and drew forth his gold. . . . How the guineas shone as they came pouring out of the dark leather mouths! . . . He loved the guineas best, but he would not change the silver—the crowns and half-crowns that were his own earnings, begotten by his labour; he loved them all. He spread them out in heaps and bathed his hands in them; then he . . . felt their rounded outline between his thumb and fingers, and thought fondly of the guineas that were only half-earned by the work in his loom, as if they had been unborn children (2: 70).

And when the gold does turn into a child, it is characteristic of Silas that he should make his decision to keep her with the words 'I can't let it go' (13: 172). Silas lives most intensely through his fingers' ends. As the narrator informs us, his is 'a clinging life' (10: 129).

George Eliot can effectively use touch as a metonymic image for sexual relations. One of the most memorable scenes in *Romola* is that in which Romola, caressing her husband, recoils at the discovery that he is wearing chain armour under his clothes (27: 381). It marks, essentially, the end of their union: the hard resisting surface that replaces the yielding and accommodating flesh is an image of some force; it becomes a lasting barrier between them emotionally and physically, and Romola is conscious of this moment as making an era in her marriage. A similar rendering of physical inflexibility as sexual rejection is the incident between Dorothea and Casaubon. Dorothea has found 'her ardour . . . continually repulsed' in their relations. This significant phrase is presently given a physical enactment when, in a moment of devotion, she takes her husband's arm:

> She turned and passed her hand through his arm.
> Mr Casaubon kept his hands behind him and allowed her

pliant arm to cling with difficulty against his rigid arm.

There was something horrible to Dorothea in the sensation which this unresponsive hardness inflicted on her. That is a strong word, but not too strong (*M*, 42: 312).

From such incidents we can draw probable conclusions as to the Casaubons' sex life. And the language continues the sexual suggestion in the imagery of spilled seed and waste land: 'it is in these acts called trivialities that the seeds of joy are forever wasted, until men and women look round with haggard faces at the devastation their own waste has made, and say, the earth bears no harvest of sweetness'.

To proceed to the consideration of taste. George Eliot, I think, is one of the more salivatory writers. Remember Maggie with her jam puff, swinging in the elder tree, 'lost to almost everything but a vague sense of jam and idleness' (*MF*, I, 6: 99); and, at Raveloe gatherings, the 'hams and chines uncut, pork-pies with the scent of the fire in them, spun butter in all its freshness' (*SM*, 3: 72). However, eating seems to be connected with children and the lower classes, the Poysers and Tullivers and Osgoods; you seldom catch the more elevated souls like Romola or Dorothea at table. But among those who enjoy their creature comforts, like Hetty and Tessa, eating often has sexual connotations. Tito wakes the peasant girl Tessa with a kiss, and then begs milk and bread of her, and then proposes another kiss (*R*, 2: 37-8). Their relation progresses with the giving and taking of food, and as with the mutual meeting of eyes we have emphasis on the shared nature of the physical experience: Tito pours 'apricots, and cakes, and comfits' into Tessa's apron, and she insists he eat some too (10: 162); then he falls asleep with his head on her lap, while 'Tessa sat quiet as a dove on its nest, just venturing, when he was fast asleep, to touch the wonderful dark curls that fell backward from his ear' (10: 167). George Eliot does not need to be more explicit than this about the nature of the subsequent sexual union, and the eggs that Tessa is to hatch in that nest.

One consumable item has particular sensual power in George Eliot's writing, perhaps because it is also a bodily fluid — milk and milk products. Right from the *Scenes of Clerical Life*, where she indulgently dwells on the sources of cream in the udders of the large sleek cows (1: 10), she is apt to rhapsodise about milk and butter, whey and cheese. The complex physical indulgence envis-

aged in consuming these has a widely-spreading set of associations: with the physical processes of generation, birth and lacta-
tion, and with moral metaphors of mother's milk and the milk of
human kindness. *Of course* dairymaids are desirable, is the
corollary — and perhaps Hardy learned that from George Eliot.
Hetty at her work of buttermaking in the dairy, as perceived by
Arthur, is part of a sensuous continuum that comprehends sight
and touch and taste and smell. She not only makes the butter: she
is the butter, eminently consumable, a smooth creamy surface of
arm and breast and milk and butter and subcutaneous fat:

> The dairy was certainly worth looking at: . . . such coolness,
> such purity, such fresh fragrance of new-pressed cheese, of firm
> butter, of wooden vessels perpetually bathed in pure water. . . .
> But one gets only a confused notion of these details when they
> surround a distractingly pretty girl of seventeen, standing on
> little pattens and rounding her dimpled arm to lift a pound of
> butter out of the scale. . . .
>   And they are the prettiest attitudes and movements into
> which a pretty girl is thrown in making up butter — tossing
> movements that give a charming curve to the arm, and a side-
> ward inclination to the round white neck; little patting and
> rolling movements with the palm of the hand. . . . And then the
> butter itself seems to communicate a fresh charm — it is so
> pure, so sweet-scented; it is turned off the mould with such a
> beautiful firm surface, like marble in a pale yellow light! (*AB*,
> 7: 127–9).

Such a passage is calculated to set the reader salivating as much as
any more overtly pornographic description in *Fanny Hill*.
   If it is Arthur the young squire who gets the cream and butter,
the carpenter Adam has to settle for whey, the leavings, as he is
to inherit Hetty after Arthur has finished with her. Adam is disposed to be satisfied, and drinks the whey eagerly before going to
meet Hetty. The narrator rhapsodises, 'Ah! I think I taste that
whey now — with a flavour so delicate that one can hardly distinguish it from an odour, and with that soft gliding warmth that
fills one's imagination with a still, happy dreaminess' (20: 263).
It's back to the breast for George Eliot's men!
   To continue my survey of the senses: the olfactory, now — what
can a novelist do with smell? George Eliot does a good deal,

though here she uses the language of the sense to convey that we should not be too finnicky with our noses. Fastidiousness as to smell is often a characteristic of her faulty women; and it also seems to imply distaste for other kinds of physical relation. Nancy Lammeter in *Silas Marner* is for the most part sympathetically handled, but her delicacy and refinement, her propensity to have everything about her smelling 'of lavender and rose-leaves' (*SM*, 11, 147), is connected with her childlessness. When we first hear Rosamond Vincy she is complaining about the smell of red herring and grilled bone (*M*, ii: 72, 74), and she is further characterised by her olfactory daintiness in being able 'to discern very subtly the faintest aroma of rank' (16: 123). She puts up with Lydgate's thick-headed cousin, because 'Captain Lydgate's stupidity was delicately scented, and carried itself with "style"' (58: 425). After insisting on riding with this delicately scented captain during her pregnancy, Rosamond has an accident that causes a miscarriage: again this sensory fastidiousness implies a life-denying revulsion from natural physical processes.

Esther Lyon is a heroine who reforms in this respect. We first hear of her as insisting on the extravagance of wax candles because she is 'so delicately framed that the smell of tallow is loathsome to her' (*FH*, 5: 140); but presently we find her willing to put up with 'the lingering odours of the early dinner' on the chance of meeting Felix Holt — a noble sacrifice that is at once rewarded, as Felix duly arrives to make 'the brothy odours endurable' (27: 358–9). Felix has already characterised himself as not being 'one of your ringed and scented men of the people' (5: 145). So Esther's moral growth, it seems, is signalled partly by her readiness to abandon her olfactory standards in favour of Felix, whose virile bodily odours are no doubt considerable. As the Reverend Mr Lyon declares sententiously, 'The scornful nostril and the high head gather not the odours that lie on the track of truth' (5: 147). There is a similar set of associations in the pathologically frigid Gwendolen Harleth. During Grandcourt's courtship she takes satisfaction that his amorous attentions are as 'inobtrusive as a wafted odour of roses' (*DD*, 29: 371).

An excessive concern for cleanliness, as an implicit denial of all strong sensation, suggests sexual sterility and death. The location in George Eliot's novels that most clearly exemplifies this alignment is Garum Firs, the house of uncle and aunt Pullet in *The Mill on the Floss*. The Pullets are childless, and likely to remain so: 'Stop the children, for God's sake, Bessy — don't let 'em come up the door-step,' cries aunt Pullet, as her sisters' children approach. Before they enter they must have their shoes wiped, an operation that Tom 'always considered in the light of an indignity to his sex' (*MF*, I, 9: 148). Aunt Pullet's obsession for cleanliness is suggestive of a fanatic chastity. The girls, as they mount the glassily polished stairs, feel that 'the ascent of these glossy steps might have served in barbarous times as a trial by ordeal from which none but the most spotless virtue could have come off with unbroken limbs' (9: 149). The imagery of virginity merges with the imagery of death: the furniture at Garum Firs 'looked like the corpses of furniture in white shrouds' (9: 150), and the event aunt Pullet looks forward to with most luxurious anticipation is her own funeral (9: 152). She is likewise the aunt who most volubly objects to the signs of Maggie's sexuality, her long hair and rounded arm.

So from the ways George Eliot's characters see, hear, touch, taste, and smell, we can learn a good deal about their moral, psychological, and sexual lives.

I proceed to an examination of some of the recurrent images by which she communicates, either overtly or covertly, the life of the body. And, since I'm dealing with animal functions, I'll begin with animals. Her novels are plentifully populated with animals, particularly dogs, who are recurrently seen as mirrors of their masters. And if the animals are like us, so are we like the animals, and our animal nature had better not be denied.

The most simply physical beings among the characters are simply called animals. Hetty is a kitten, Tessa is a 'pigeon', and a 'puss-faced minx', and she makes companions of young goats. The sexual life of such beings is not difficult to deduce: they go to it like the wren and the small gilded fly. In the case of more complex consciousnesses, however, the analogies are not so direct. We must gather a good deal about Arthur Donnithorne's alternation between conscience and 'unbridled passion', as the novels say, by his behaviour with his horse.[6] He consistently works off his sexual passion by bestriding a horse, a female one if possible. When he is tempted to waylay Hetty in the wood, he resolves instead to ride off to Eagledale on his mare Meg. 'Well, Meg, my pretty girl', he promises her amorously, 'we'll have a glorious canter this morning.' When it emerges that Meg is lame, the usually good-humoured Arthur swears at his groom, and 'considered himself thoroughly disappointed and annoyed' (12: 172). Balked of the mare, he goes for a gallop on Rattler; but the gelding proves to be not efficacious in allaying his passion, and presently he is galloping back to be on time to meet Hetty in the wood after all: 'ridin' the devil's own pace', as the coachman observes (12: 173).

After his violent encounter with Adam, Arthur is forced to consider giving up Hetty for good. The only way he can contemplate such a thing is by turning again to his other female, Meg. It is a loving encounter:

> Once on Meg's back . . . he should be more master of the situation.
> The pretty creature arched her bay neck in the sunshine, and pawed the gravel, and trembled with pleasure when her master stroked her nose, and patted her, and talked to her even in a more caressing tone than usual (29: 360).

His fierce gallop this time seems to work, as he is able to resolve to drop Hetty. But his fiery passions are hard on Meg, as they have been hard on Hetty: 'He's been ridin' fit to split the mare i' two', complains the groom (24: 362). D.H. Lawrence, who goes in for men on mares and boys on rocking horses, can hardly offer more explicit imagery. Like Mr Rochester — whom Jane Eyre first thought to be a gytrash — Arthur is equine, a stud, a composite of man and horse in which the horse, this great beast between his legs, recurrently suggests his vigorous sexuality. The narrator at one point ironically considers the centaur in connection with Arthur's propensity to work off his temptations by hard riding: 'Nothing like "taking" a few bushes and ditches for exorcising a demon; and it is really astonishing that the Centaurs, with their immense advantages in this way, have left so bad a reputation in history' (12: 173). Sublimation, as the psychiatrists have discovered, doesn't always work.

Riding is recurrently linked with sexuality in George Eliot's novels, for the women as for the men. It is characteristic of the immature, self-repressive Dorothea that she should enjoy riding 'in a pagan sensuous way', and that she should therefore look forward to renouncing it (*M*, 1: 7). (I confess I always wish George Eliot had shown Dorothea going for a good gallop with Will Ladislaw at the end — if possible, while wearing her emeralds!) Gwendolen on horseback is conscious of an intoxicating access of

power: 'that utmost excitement of the coming chase which consists in feeling something like a combination of dog and horse,
with the super-added thrill . . . of centaur-power' (*DD*, 7: 102).
As a female centaur, she is another composite of woman and
beast, temptress and destroyer, like the siren Becky Sharp in
Vanity Fair. In this hunting episode she is literally and figura-
tively the downfall of her amorous cousin Rex.

How would Victorian heroines have got on without their pets, I
wonder? Dickens was well aware of the sexual suggestiveness of
Dora's Gyp, Florence Dombey's Diogenes, Pet Meagles' Lion. The
attendant animal becomes a kind of mediator through which the
chaste heroine may be closely approached by her suitor. The imagery is with us still in magazines and television commercials, in
which ladies stroke Persian cats or Afghan hounds before enamoured males. George Eliot has one developed incident in which
the caressing of an animal becomes a means of illicit sexual com-
munication. Stephen Guest has sought out Maggie one evening
when he knows Lucy will be out, and the two are intensely conscious of being alone together for the first time. Maggie is holding
Minny, the little King Charles spaniel, and Stephen leans towards
her to stroke 'the long curly ears':

> It seems to Stephen like some action in a dream that he was ob-
> liged to do, and wonder at himself all the while — to go on
> stroking Minny's head. . . . As for Maggie she had no distinct
> thought — only a sense of a presence like that of a closely-hover-
> ing broad-winged bird in the darkness, for she was unable to
> look up and saw nothing but Minny's black wavy coat (III, 6:
> 519).

Are we to infer some heavy sexual symbolism, that will make
Minny the 'pussy' that the male caresses? Not necessarily. But we
do have a scene that is charged with sexual excitement.

Human hair, like animal fur, does duty as sexual symbol in
George Eliot's novels. Here again Maggie is our chief example.
Her unruly dark hair is like so many of her attributes, including
her sexuality — both an asset and a disability. 'I think the gell has
too much hair', says her fastidious aunt Pullet. 'I'd have it
thinned and cut shorter, sister, if I was you: it isn't good for her
health. It's that as makes her skin so brown, I shouldn't wonder'
(*MF*, I, 7: 118). She sounds like Dr Acton discoursing on the dire

effects of masturbation.[7] It is this speech that drives Maggie to her daring resolution to do away with her hair and her woman's disability at the same time, and cut it off — an action that relates her to numbers of other heroines whose hair is symbolic of their sex, like Rapunzel, Belinda (whose lock is raped), Jo in *Little Women*, and Anne of Green Gables. Romola too is related to Rapunzel, as a girl who reaches maturity in a seclusion so complete that she has never seen a young man at close quarters until Tito arrives. And she too is identified for us and for surrounding characters by her hair. The 'glimmering of something bright', her golden hair, is the last thing her father is able to perceive before total blindness overtakes him (*R*, 3: 60). The lovemaking between her and Tito is usually rendered by accounts of their merging hair: at their first kiss 'the dark curls mingled for an instant with the rippling gold' (12: 184). And presently they are presented, 'she with her long white hands on the dark-brown curls, and he with his dark fingers bathed in the streaming gold' (17: 270). The imagery is perhaps a touch banal. But George Eliot adds piquancy by her irony — showing how Romola discovers that her husband has been giving locks of his hair to Tessa too:

> When the curl was held towards her, it seemed for an instant like a mocking phantasm of the lock she herself had cut to wind with her own five years ago. . . .
> 'It is a beautiful curl,' she said, resisting the impulse to withdraw her hand (*R*, 56: 267).

Romola's registering of her husband's infidelity is sufficiently though reticently conveyed by that last phrase.

Will Ladislaw's hair, which like Romola's is a source of light, is one of his prominent physical attractions: 'When he turned his head quickly his hair seemed to shake out light', Dorothea notices; and by his side Mr Casaubon stands 'rayless' (*M*, 21: 155). His particular dread is of becoming 'ray-shorn' in her eyes: a term that neatly connects his Apollonian attribute of enlightenment with his hair and his potency. Grandcourt's baldness is perhaps a feature that makes Gwendolen not recognise him as a sexual threat.

To move from hair to other parts of the body: Goerge Eliot, I think, was an arm woman. For her characters the generalised desire of the flesh is particularly located in the arm. Hetty, the most purely physical creature in the novels, is characterised by 'her dimpled arm', the 'charming curve to [her] arm', and so forth. Arms are the sexual medium between her and her two men: Arthur's first unmistakable sexual advance is to lay 'his hand on the soft arm that was nearest to him' (12: 177). Adam, himself a fine physical specimen with 'an arm that was likely to win the prize for feats of strength' (1: 50), also courts her by a process of wooing her arms. 'Such big arms as mine were made for little arms like yours to lean on', he coaxes her, as he carries her basket of cherries (20: 267). Her arms are to Hetty herself the synecdoche for her whole physical being. When she has decided not to drown herself, she celebrates her new lease on life by '[turning] up her sleeves, and [kissing] her arms with the passionate love of life' (37: 433).

The intense desirableness of a woman's arm is registered again in the scene in *The Mill on the Floss* where Stephen compulsively kisses Maggie's arm:

> Who has not felt the beauty of a woman's arm? — the unspeakable suggestions of tenderness that lie in the dimpled elbow and all the varied gently lessening curves down to the delicate wrist with its tiniest, almost imperceptible nicks in the firm softness (*MF*, iii, 10: 561).

Well might the *Saturday Review* critic pick out this scene for special objection.[8]

In rereading the novels for the purpose of writing this paper I confess to having found sex in almost everything. Yes, even the vegetables. George Eliot, the daughter of a timber-valuer, endows trees with passion, and sometimes suggests in the very landscape a potency for copulation. Arthur, filled with the idea of Hetty, finds the 'beeches and smooth limes' too inflammatory, and flees to the safer masculine company of 'the strong knotted old oaks' (*AB*, 13: 183). And Adam has been looking intently at 'a curious large beech' which has the aspect of 'two trees wedded together'[9] immediately before he sees Arthur and Hetty kissing in the wood. At the opening of *The Mill on the Floss* does not the scene invite us to consider the wedding of tide with sea, and to envisage some loving conjunction between masculine fir-planks and feminine sacks?

A wide plain, where the broadening Floss hurries on between its green banks to the sea, and the loving tide, rushing to meet it, checks its passage with an impetuous embrace. On this mighty tide the black ships — laden with the fresh-scented fir-planks, with rounded sacks of oil-bearing seed, or with the dark glitter of coal — are borne along to the town of St Ogg's (*MF*, I, 1: 53).

George Eliot's landscapes are not less fertilely suggestive than Hardy's, which are even scattered with phallic pebbles: at Flint-comb-Ash Tess works in fields which are covered with 'loose white flints in bulbous, cusped, and phallic shapes' (ch. 43). I was relieved to discover, after poring over the complex sexual sugges-tiveness of the scenes of the Red Deeps in *The Mill*, that that piece of landscape had prompted a whole chapter by Ellen Moers on female sexual symbolism.[10]

Though the restrictions of her day precluded the direct and literal description of sexual relations, George Eliot is nonetheless able to convey all she needs by shifting to the figurative level. And her power of imagining and rendering even abnormal sexual relations through imagery is considerable. From the imagery we can deduce a great deal about the burnt-out adulterous passion between Mrs Transome and the sleek Jermyn, the horrible inter-action of frigidity and sadism in the Grandcourt marriage, and the combination of deprivation and exploitation in the Casaubon marriage. In the last we are presented almost with the monstrous, a copulation of pen and ink with living human flesh to produce an inhuman offspring. Mr Casaubon's blood, as Mrs Cadwallader reports, examined under a microscope, turns out to be 'all semicolons and parentheses' (8: 52). As a conscientious husband he recognises his duty to leave after him 'a copy of himself'; but the copy he has in mind is 'of his mythological key' (29: 205). By feverish midnight activity in the bedroom he does what he can to impregnate his wife with his key, working with 'bird-like speed' (48: 349) like a lecherous sparrow. The posthumous offspring of this coupling, an 'embryo of truth' (48: 351), will result for Dorothea in 'a ghastly labour producing what would never see the light' (48: 348), 'a theory which was already withered in the birth like an elfin child' (48: 351). The imagery of coition, labour and parturition here suggests something more than the literal and the physical, evoking the terrified fantasies of a tormented psyche.[11]

If sex does not occupy the foreground of George Eliot's novels — if it doesn't 'take the outside place in the presentation', as it does in Hardy's and Lawrence's — it is not because she has censored it out. The physical and sexual lives of her characters are very fully expressed, albeit often by indirection. By moving the depiction of sex from the literal to the figurative level she has not only satisfied a prudish readership, but created a range of expression that can be more powerful than direct statement.

NOTES

1   I use the following editions of George Eliot's novels, with title abbreviations as indicated: *Scenes of Clerical Life* (*SCL*) ed. David Lodge (Harmondsworth: Penguin Books, 1973); *Adam Bede* (*AB*), ed. Stephen Gill (Harmondsworth: Penguin Books, 1980); *The Mill on the Floss* (*MF*), ed. A.S. Byatt (Harmondsworth: Penguin Books, 1979); *Silas Marner* (*SM*), ed. Q.D. Leavis (Harmondsworth: Penguin Books 1967); *Romola*, vols 19 and 20 of the Cabinet Edition of *The Works of George Eliot*, 24 vols (Edinburgh and London: William Blackwood and Sons, 1878–); *Felix Holt* (*FH*), ed. Peter Coveney (Harmondsworth: Penguin Books 1972); *Middlemarch* (*M*), ed. Gordon S. Haight (Boston: Houghton Mifflin, 1956); *Daniel Deronda* (*DD*), ed. Barbara Hardy (Harmondsworth: Penguin Books, 1967). References, which are included in the text, are by chapter and page number.
2   Unsigned review, *Saturday Review*, 7 (26 February 1859), 250–51. See *George Eliot: The Critical Heritage*, ed. David Carroll (London: Routledge and Kegan Paul, 1971), p. 76.
3   *British Quarterly Review*, 45 (January 1867), 164.
4   'Incest Patterns in Two Victorian Novels,' *Literature and Psychology*, 15 (Summer 1965), 155.
5   *Saturday Review*, 9 (14 April 1860), 470–1. See *George Eliot: The Critical Heritage*, p. 118. See also Ruskin's severe comments on 'the English Cockney school, which consummates itself in George Eliot', *Critical Heritage*, p. 166–7.
6   The narrator early establishes a connection between horses and passion in referring to 'heroes fiery horses, themselves ridden by still more fiery passions' (3: 82). Although these heroes are the stereotypes that the narrator professes *not* to be writing about, it is clear that Arthur views himself as a hero of this species: 'Arthur felt himself very heroic as he strode towards the stables to give his orders about the horses' (12: 169).
7   For example: 'The frame is stunted and weak, the muscles undeveloped, the eye is sunken and heavy, the complexion is sallow.' William Acton, *The Functions and Disorders of the Reproductive Organs* (1857), as quoted by Stephen Marcus, *The Other Victorians* (New York: Basic Books, 1964), p. 19.
8   *Saturday Review*, 9 (14 April 1860), 471.

9   Thus in the first and most subsequent editions. The Penguin edition reads 'two trees welded together' (27: 341).

10 *Literary Women* (Garden City, NY: Doubleday, 1972), pp. 65, 243–64.

11 See also David Carroll, '*Middlemarch* and the Externality of Fact', in Ian Adam, ed., *This Particular Web: Essays on Middlemarch* (Toronto: University of Toronto Press, 1975), p. 85; and A.L. French, 'A Note on *Middlemarch*,' *Nineteenth-Century Fiction*, 26:3 (December 1971), 339–46. Professor French, in discussing a single passage in *Middlemarch* to show its sexual and psychological implications, has done what I have audaciously tried to do for the novels at large–that is, he shows how in George Eliot's novels 'we are to hear one thing talked of in terms of another' (p. 341).

3 A Meredithian Glance at Gwendolen Harleth

ELIZABETH A. DANIELS

Even though they were poles apart in some respects, George Eliot and George Meredith profit by comparison in relation to their views on women. Between 1872 and 1885 there were four significant novels about women by these two most important novelists of the late Victorian period. George Eliot's *Middlemarch* (1872) was followed by her last novel *Daniel Deronda* (1876). George Meredith's *The Egoist* (1879) was written three years later and followed by *Diana of the Crossways* (1885). Certain attitudes towards women reflected in these four novels are very similar.

Their central themes in each case were a concern for the intellectual, moral, and emotional development of women. Both writers came out of the same context. The Teufelsdröckhian backdrop of the quest for the realisation of male selfhood was a central controlling literary image of the period, balanced against the notion of the 'angel in the house', the Victorian wife who ministers to her husband, her children, and her household. In this context in which the very idea of experience was considered unwomanly, each author tackled questions of women's experience, especially married women's experience, as one of the major themes of the novels. For different reasons, neither of them wished to overturn the institution of marriage, but separately, each was sharply critical of the callousness and deadness which surrounded the woman's role in Victorian marriage, and of the male egoism which was its backbone. Both believed that women must rise to flourish at the same intellectual level as men and must learn to be realists, counteracting the inanity and passivity of Philistinism and sentimentalism which were at the heart of Victorian custom. They believed also that society needed and would benefit from the encouragement of women's fullest psychic development, and that their psychic development was in some ways different from men's, but no less deep, and not inferior.

It is not, in George Eliot's case, until *Daniel Deronda* is considered in a context with its predecessor *Middlemarch*, on the one hand, and Meredith's novels of the next decade, on the other, that the ever-unresolved conflicts of George Eliot about women seem to tip so sharply towards a modern scepticism and alienation. Except for *Daniel Deronda*, indeed, no one of George Eliot's novels leaves today's readers with the sense that the emotional and psychical repercussions of women's repression are permanently debilitating. In this novel, however, there is no longer what I would call a false resolution of the woman's struggle for self-development. This pattern is breaking up in the world of Gwendolen Harleth, who never has any interest in ministering to her husband Grandcourt, but, once awakened, begins a search for the roots of her own conscience, which she is unable to complete because of failures in the system and shallowness in herself.

A pervasive feeling of ambiguity and futility about women's efforts, together with an accompanying sense of powerlessness and psychological distress, seem to me to sound a new and changed note in this last novel of George Eliot, the only one placed in a contemporary setting. The final words of Gwendolen's letter to Daniel Deronda on his wedding day affirm her desire for self-hood and service. But the tears, fears, sleeplessness, hysteria, and nightmares that have ripped apart her psyche belie the affirmation. Such a configuration places the final George Eliot heroine as transitional, in strong kinship with her Meredithian sister to follow in the same decade and accordingly somewhat out of phase with her antecedents. The fragmented and destructive forces still present in Gwendolen's mind at our last glimpse of it permit us to classify Gwendolen as a precursor of first Meredith's and then Hardy's unsettled modern women, plagued by conflicts and unresolved questions, desiring to gain their identities but powerless to control their courses.

The theme insurgent in all Meredith's novels to follow is the rising need for women to break through their customary patterns of submission to male domination ('egoism', as he puts it) and, taking courage, experiment — growing and learning to become the controllers of their own destinies. Before they can do so, however, they often must suffer psychic breakdown or psychic stress

(as in *The Amazing Marriage, Lord Ormont and His Aminta,* or
The Egoist). Their debasing attitudes towards self must be
uprooted, and new ones developed to take their place. Slowly
learning to recognise and acknowledge their own feelings and
goals, women learn to arrange themselves anew, releasing themselves from their former complete dependence on men. In due
course the cumulative energies unleashed in the individual
transformations of countless women will result in the transformation of society, Meredith believes. 'It is the new energy seen in
women', he wrote in 1907 in an unpublished letter to Eleanor O.
Brownell, now in possession of the author, 'that gives me hope for
the future.'

Meredith foretold, however, that the liberating development of
women could only be accomplished in society if men too were
liberated — that is, if men played a non-stereotypical role in help-
ing the women to find themselves and broaden their experience.
Yet the typical Victorian egoistic male in Meredith's view was probably incapable of such understanding and sympathy. Therefore,
a new enlightenment in men as well as women must be brought
about. The laws, the customs, the educational systems must all
give way. Since most men were not ready for this reformed society,
Meredith's heroines were often studied portraits of victims and
ingenues, trying to find their ways out of traps baited by men.

I have said all this about Meredith as prelude to my discussion
of George Eliot because I find the interconnections between their
thought the key to a changing strain in George Eliot which has
been somewhat overlooked. Philip Wakem's relationship with
Maggie, Ladislaw's relationship with the married Dorothea, and
finally Klesmer's and Daniel Deronda's relationship with
Gwendolen *all* precede Meredith's conception of Vernon Whit-
ford, the disinterested adviser of Clara Middleton. These
Meredithian and Eliotian men seem to me to be placed in their
respective novels for precisely the same purpose — to assist and
prod the heroine in breaking her bonds with her past, to serve as
an 'outer conscience'.[1] With George Eliot, as with Meredith, the
issue of women's repression in the male egoistic system is of rising
importance as her thought develops. In her earlier novels George
Eliot still insists that women can and must accommodate themselves to the fixed limitations of the system. Within it, they can
find a way to make constructive use of their talents. They can do
so chiefly through deepening their education and thus their
moral understanding. She writes to John Morley in May 1867:

[T]hroughout all transitions, the goal towards which we are proceeding is a more clearly discerned distinction of function . . . with as near an approach to equivalence of good for woman and for man as can be secured by the effort of growing moral force to lighten the pressure of hard non-moral outward conditions.

In fact, gradually, and with the moral evolution which she believes is at work, 'nature' will be 'mended' ('in the moral evolution we have an art which does mend nature. . . ').[2] Although the external world seems to present an immutable necessity, as human beings develop their moral systems, they can modify the natural system. To figure out where it admits of modification is the most important sphere of human activity.

Until *Daniel Deronda*, then, George Eliot does not seem prepared to admit that under the Victorian code and in Victorian society, women's altruistic sacrifices are sometimes fruitless in lightening the pressure of 'hard non-moral outward conditions'.

But in *Daniel Deronda* it appears that George Eliot has finally come nearer to this harsher conclusion. The tensions which she has subdued in Maggie and ironically reconciled in Dorothea and Mary Garth refuse to be dispelled or subsumed as this final novel comes to a close. Although Gwendolen will try to overcome her disaffection with moral force and learn to fit herself into the conventions of the system, there are severely conditioning forces at work which she may not be able to control. Gwendolen is led by Daniel Deronda to believe that she can find herself among the pieces of her fragmented experience, put herself back together again, and then get on with the business of being a better woman as he would define one. What actually goes on in Gwendolen's mind at the end of the book, however, tends to suggest that even though wishing to, she may not be able to succeed, and that she may well be emotionally and intellectually, if not morally, crippled for life.

Gwendolen Harleth is deeply injured by her experience with Grandcourt. The enlarging of her 'narrow round' (36: 507), as Daniel Deronda puts it, starts problematically late and brings neither liberation nor resignation. She is patently neurotic and has been totally miseducated. While Deronda, in tones which inspire confidence, assures Gwendolen that if she confronts her past fears and misactions, especially her immoral decision to get married, she can learn to be better, he has not heard her fits of shrieking which, as the reader can only guess, may not abate. It seems entirely possible that George Eliot intended such negative ambiguity and uncertainty as to Gwendolen's fate, since she left so many unresolved loose ends in the novel. At its beginning Gwendolen is a young egoist — self-indulgent and interested only in advancing herself. Like Rosamond a rather pitiable product of her system, she has never taken life very seriously. A spoiled child, she has grown up to be a spoiled woman. Unaware of the social and altruistic implications of life, she has some talents but she has misappropriated her energy and intelligence. The gambling in her blood is really boredom. She has no centre and has not found the 'root' of her own 'conscience' (54: 733) because she has never been concerned to look for it:

> She rejoiced to feel herself exceptional, but her horizon was that of the genteel romance where the heroine's soul poured out in her journal is full of vague power, originality, and general rebellion, while her life moves strictly in the sphere of fashion; and if she wanders into a swamp, the pathos lies partly, so to speak, in her having on her satin shoes. Here is a restraint which nature and society have provided on the pursuit of striking adventure; so that a soul burning with a sense of what the universe is not, and ready to take all existence as fuel, is nevertheless held captive by the ordinary wirework of social forms and does nothing particular (6: 83).

Gwendolen enters into the gamble of a relationship with Grandcourt, an equally autocratic and completely ruthless, unprincipled male egoist. In doing so, she knowingly commits an ethical crime, hardly to be avoided, however, under Victorian marriage laws. Breaking faith with a promise she has made to Lydia Glasher, Grandcourt's mistress, she marries Grandcourt, aware that Lydia's son will miss his chance of an inheritance from Grandcourt if Grandcourt and she, his legal wife, have a son. Even so, she justifies the decision to marry by convincing herself that it is necessary for her mother's economic welfare.

Like Dorothea's and Casaubon's marriage in *Middlemarch*, the relationship that develops becomes the ironical antithesis of a satisfactory marriage. On her part, Gwendolen has entered into this marriage as a wilful act of egoism, knowing that she was frigid and not in the least interested in giving herself to another human being. Grandcourt is determined to bend the will of his wife and yet continue, as usual, his alternate relationship with his mistress.

Deep into the heart of the action of this bifurcated novel, Gwendolen has become not only alienated but murderous. At that point she has come to realise that to marry Grandcourt was an utter mistake. Gradually, over a period of time, Gwendolen has developed such a hatred and fear of Grandcourt that she begins to wish for him to die. She sees his dead white face everywhere both before and after he dies in a sailboat accident. When he has drowned, obsessed with guilty knowledge, she knows that in her thoughts and possibly in her actions, she is a murderer. Although she has not been responsible for his going overboard, she has failed to throw him the rope that was available, so eager was she that he should perish. This guilt weighs heavily on her soul.

Before his death, Grandcourt has had a growing suspicion, in which he was somewhat although not entirely mistaken, that Gwendolen was trying to have an affair with Deronda. In fact, she had really only approached Deronda for advice, having realised upon first acquaintance when he returned her necklace to her at the gambling casino, that he was someone with deep sympathy and understanding. In turn, Deronda had demonstrated an immediate curiosity about her which developed into a warm friendliness. Gwendolen has slowly moved towards Deronda and, through him, has begun to gain some insight into herself, something that had never really happened to her before.

Since Daniel is an atypical male, the idealised opposite of a Victorian male egoist, he is capable of standing aside from the system to see what is going on and offering her sympathetic but disinterested advice. Brought up as Sir Hugo Mallinger's ward, he has always felt set apart, even before he knew he was Jewish. Because of his abstraction from Victorian convention and custom, he is a perfect vehicle to help Gwendolen step aside to get her bearing and see who she is.

Daniel Deronda has served Gwendolen as adviser after her confidence in herself has been not only completely shaken, but turned to remorse and dread:

This hidden helplessness gave fresh force to the hold Deronda had from the first taken on her mind, as one who had an unknown standard by which he judged her. Had he some way of looking at things which might be a new footing for her — an inward safeguard against possible events which she dreaded as stored-up retribution? (35: 484).

Deronda had lit up her attention with a sense of novelty: not by words only, but by imagined facts, his influence had entered into the current of that self-suspicion and self-blame which awakens a new consciousness (35: 485).

For her he has played the triple role of confessor, absolver, and teacher. When she has told him that her life seems pointless and stale, he has suggested a way that life could be made to seem 'worth more' (36: 507). She must broaden her experience, he says, get out of herself. 'It is the curse of your life . . . of so many lives, that all passion is spent in that narrow round [of egotism] for want of ideas and sympathies to make a larger home for it' (36: 507). Her failure has been inexperience and passivity — she is so ignorant that she has nothing to go on. She must cast loose and think of a way to establish her own meaning. 'I will try', she says. 'I will think' (36: 508).

'Think' is the key word in this relationship. As Deronda has suggested, Gwendolen has lived on whims and excuses and catered to her own fears and weaknesses. Now what she needs to do is to stop making excuses for herself, and instead, make the attempt to find her conscience and redirect herself. 'Take the present suffering as a painful letting in of light', he tells her. 'You are conscious of more beyond the round of your own inclinations — you know more of the way in which your life presses on others, and their life on yours. I don't think you could have escaped the painful process in some form or other' (36: 508).

And so with rudimentary psychotherapy Deronda attempts a cure. But Gwendolen does not respond as expected. She is so obsessed with her own sense of guilt that she cannot quickly change her bias. And Daniel, while helpful, has his own fate to work out. He has already gone through a similar painful process to that which Gwendolen must go through before she can prove herself. As he has taught Gwendolen to do, he has found out the facts about himself, including at length the providential information imparted by his mother, who summoned him to her side in Italy. His ordering of facts will permit him to work out a calling in the East. He will create a new society for Jews — an ideal state founded upon an abstract idea. Thus he will construct and direct his own experience. No such luck for Gwendolen.

One thing neither Gwendolen nor Deronda had counted on was that she would lean on him so hard that she would begin to assume that the relationship would lead to marriage (there being no other valid form of permanent close friendship between men and women). He had not told Gwendolen of Mirah, his intended, as their relationship grew. Consequently, the light net of hope that Gwendolen wove in her mind around her relationship with Deronda immediately unravelled when she learned of her delusion. Not free of the guilt of her past, weak from the chaos of her inner turmoil, with no sustaining dream of the future, she was apparently left in a state of collapse — a pitiable bundle of conflicts. As Henry James observed, she was punished for being narrow, but she was not allowed to expand.[3] One finishes this book recognising how strongly George Eliot must have resented the waste in the mordant stifling of the energies of women in her times.

Daniel Deronda is a very different marriage book from *Middlemarch* to which it is nevertheless most closely akin in George Eliot's rubric. In *Middlemarch* Dorothea knows full well that she is married to a moral blind man and a dry-as-dust scholar, but she accepts her role and tries to work within it. In *Daniel Deronda* the situation is less tenable. The furies of Gwendolen's mind have begun to pull it apart. The course of her experience in the book has been the unrolling of negatives. She has learned that she can't pursue music because her voice is not good enough; she has failed to find a positive basis in her marriage. She has realised how ignorant and unself-knowing she is. She has experienced terror and fear in trying to face the truth about herself and her motivation, and she has at no time been able to make creative use of her own powers. She has been self-deluding, cowardly, and internally violent. To cap the climax, she has leaned on a mentor of great promise only to have him extract himself from her periphery before she is ready to carry on effectively the task of self-knowledge he has assigned her.

Looked at in this light, the plight of George Eliot's last heroine is somewhat baffling and certainly uncharacteristic. The rationalists Deronda and Mordecai may in fact be able to found the futurist Zionist state, drawn up flawlessly in their model.

Gwendolen and her sisters, on the other hand, will have to struggle further just to rid themselves of their inappropriate satin shoes
before they can take to a similar highway of experience. But it is
clear that that is what George Eliot thinks must happen as she
forces Gwendolen to stay with her struggle.

One final comment about the new tone of alienation and bit-
terness in *Daniel Deronda*. George Eliot complements the situation of Gwendolen with a vignette of Leonora Halm-Eberstein,
Deronda's mother, who had not wanted to marry and only did so
to gain mastery over her life. She has no love for nor emotional
commitment to Deronda, and in that sense by either Christian or
Jewish standards has been a very abnormal mother. Deronda had
been brought into the world under her 'strange mental conflict'.
The Princess created for herself an anomalous freedom, and like
George Eliot, developed an insulated system in which it was
possible for her to flourish as an artist, to let her genius thrive and
not be stifled by convention. When the Princess calls her son to
her as she lies dying, and tells him of his Jewishness, she has to
admit that her social abstraction and isolation have cut her off
from ties that spell the meaning of life. But that is the bind, she
says to Deronda and the world at large, that life arranges for
woman:

> You are not a woman. You may try—but you can never ima-
> gine what it is to have a man's force of genius in you, and yet to
> suffer the slavery of being a girl. To have a pattern cut
> out—'this is the Jewish woman; this is what you must be; this is
> what you are wanted for; a woman's heart must be of such a
> size and no larger, else it must be pressed small, like Chinese
> feet; her happiness is to be made as cakes are, by a fixed re-
> ceipt'.

Displaying this attitude, the Princess may well be the most
unusual woman that George Eliot created. Not coherently connected with the substance of the novel, her presence in it nevertheless serves as an 'emblem'[4] of the suppressed conflicts that
continued unexpectedly to lie unresolved under the surface of
George Eliot's customarily more restrained statements about
women.

It was not until after many Meredithian heroines had escaped
over willow-patterned bridges with new men who stayed with

them, or, closer to Gwendolen's plight, suffered nervous break-downs and psychic disruptions, and paid other heavy emotional penalties for their struggle to come alive, that women could be freer to gain the control and command sought after but incompletely realised in Gwendolen Harleth's moral and intellectual therapy.

NOTES

1   George Eliot, *Daniel Deronda*, ed. Barbara Hardy (Harmondsworth: Penguin Books, 1967), 64: 833.
2   *The George Eliot Letters*, ed. Gordon S. Haight, 9 vols (New Haven: Yale University Press, 1954–78), v, 364.
3   Henry James, 'Daniel Deronda: A Conversation', in *Partial Portraits* (New York: Macmillan, 1919), pp. 89–90.
4   I owe this word to a colleague, Joanne Long, whose use of it in connexion with George Eliot's technique will be apparent in her yet unpublished thesis.

4 *Middlemarch* and the New Humanity

RUTH apROBERTS

In the face of some recent studies which perceive continuities from the Romantics through the Victorians to the modern, Michael Timko proposes a new view of the 'charter' or 'style' of the Victorian period as distinctively its own.[1] First, as has been rather generally observed, the Victorian age marks a more evolved self-consciousness, as the first age of 'transition', 'between two worlds', and this self-consciousness lends urgency to self-definition. Second, says Timko, and this has *not* been so generally observed, it is an age in which epistemological concerns take precedence over metaphysical. Third, Darwinism (understood as pre-Darwinian), forces a new confrontation of nature and a redefinition of humanity in its 'natural' context. In the 1830s, Timko observes, Kant's line of thought seemed to be taking hold, putting 'Natural Theology' in doubt, and insisting on solipsistic and cultural limits to our knowledge. Kant contrasts *phenomena* — données in space and time, knowable to our senses — with *noumena* — things in themselves such as ethics or ultimate reality, which we cannot know. Coleridge is concerned with how *phenomena* and *noumena* can be brought together. The Victorian concern is *whether* they can be brought together. Timko writes:

> Wordsworth's metaphysical certainty — his equating naturalistic revelation — simply is no longer possible in the Victorian period, which had come to question not how man was related to nature or God, but if in fact he could come to know anything at all, including his own place in the scheme of things, and if there were either a God or nature in the sense the Romantics had thought of them (p. 612).

The question is not how to discover the self, but *whether* the self can be discovered.

Natural science effects the second change. Nature for Wordsworth could be benign, 'The guide, the guardian of my heart, and soul / Of all my moral being'. But in the new Darwinian Nature, the nightmare vision of inexorable pitiless process — in geology, in biology, in astronomy — man cannot bear to feel himself a mere part of *that*. An early sonnet of Arnold's, that Timko refers to, faces the issue: 'To an Independent Preacher, who preached that we should be 'In Harmony with Nature':

> Know, man hath all which Nature hath, but more,
> And in that *more* lie all his hopes of good.
> Nature is cruel, man is sick of blood;
> Nature is stubborn, man would fain adore;
> Nature is fickle, man hath need of rest;
> Nature forgives no debt, and fears no grave;
> Man would be mild, and with safe conscience blest.
> Man must begin, know this, where Nature ends. . . . [2]

An extreme anxiety arises, to define humankind as separate from this nightmare nature, as something more than or different from the rest of the beasts. The Victorian mission appears to be, then, to define and assert man's humanness. It is Tennyson who says, 'I believe in God, not from what I see in Nature but from what I find in man'. For man appears to be uniquely capable of morality, which marks his 'sociality', and his 'civilization'. 'Civilization', writes Cassirer, 'constitutes no secondary or accidental characteristic but marks man's essential nature, his specific character'. Or, as Carlyle had already said,

> To understand man, we must look beyond the individual man and his actions and interests, and view him in combination with his fellows. It is in Society that man first feels what he is; first becomes what he can be. [3]

Victorian epistemology, then, looks to man in his social, distinctively human aspect.

Continental developments endorse this emphasis of Timko's. In connection with George Eliot, one thinks first of her well-established base in Comte's Positivism. Comte's three-stage theory of history — theological, metaphysical, and positive — constitutes a solid paradigm for the Victorian shift, and his invention of 'sociology' and of the non-theistic 'religion of humanity' marks the new emphasis. Comte, however, is rather unsatisfactory. Carlyle is incensed by the complacency of quantitative utilitarian Positivism; Mill objects to Comte's idea of science: phrenology, for instance, rather than the much needed psychology. And Comte's anti-protestant, pro-Catholic bias makes for a pretty poor kind of atheism. The enormously influential Carlyle made current the more satisfactory, more humane German line of thought that developed from Vico through Herder to Goethe, Wilhelm von Humboldt, and Niebuhr. (Both Vico and Herder were saints, incidentally, in the positivist calendar.) Vico's cyclical theory of history, which influenced Comte, comes out in Herder's *Historicism* as a sort of spiral — in which societies are continually changing, growing and declining and giving way to new more developed forms, each more or less fulfilling itself in its own context. *Entwicklung*, or *Development*, is the principle of change in this new Herderian anthropologic theory of history. This flux of change and the implied relativism, this process, and the idea of a *Zeitgeist* as various, variable, and yet imperious, all tend to produce a sort of cultural vertigo. Herder brings stability out of the vertiginous flow of history with his concept of *Humanität*: humanity is characterised by an infinite *potential* — it is this above all which distinguishes man from the animals. The more evolved self-consciousness of man enables him to perceive possibilities in his being, and to develop himself, infinitely. The capacity for language is at the root of humanness. Language is by definition a highly social phenomenon, and it alone makes religion possible, and all other human institutions. The individual man has a long childhood, for there is much to learn — the whole symbol system of his culture and all mankind's past, to build on.

> Who among mortals can say that he will reach or has reached the pure image of man that lies in him? . . . Every beast attains what his organization can attain; man only reaches it not, because his end is so high, so extensive, so infinite, and he begins on this earth so low, so late, and with so many external and internal obstacles.[4]

His striving against the obstacles is the essence of the great concept of *Bildung*, developed by Herder, Goethe, and Humboldt, the concept of the harmonious cultivation of all aspects of our humanness, which inspired German education, and through Carlyle and Arnold, radically shaped Victorian thought. *Bildung* is inwardness, a self-cultivation, that yields in time to vocation, engagement, in the interests of bringing about a more human and more humane society. Carlyle first made all this German theory available to George Eliot, and it further modifies the dryness of Comtism as she becomes more familiar with Lewes and with Germany. Beyond her translating of Strauss and Feuerbach, it is to be remembered that she worked with Lewes on his biography of Goethe, and did the translation of his citations from the German.

The humanity-concern Timko illustrates as a connecting idea in figures as various as Carlyle, Tennyson, Browning, Arnold, Clough, Huxley, Morris, and Ruskin. It gives rise to new genres: the Romantic subjective lyric, asserting the solitary *I am*, yields to the Victorian dialectic of *Who am I?*, or *Am I?* — Carlyle's dialectic in *Sartor* of editor and edited, Clough's *Dipsychus* or the double psyche, Tennyson's 'Two Voices'.

The idea of this epistemological-humanity concern as the 'charter' of Victorian literature, it seems to me, absolutely cries out to be connected to the flowering of the *novel* — the Victorian novel, which as I think gets its greatest impetus from just this epistemological concern, and which most elaborately and magnificently fulfils it, with great full moving worlds of whole societies, and layers and webs of interacting individuals. *Bleak House* must be one of the most virtuoso — for, I think, the greatest throng of characters with the most interlinkings. Carlyle had told about the destitute Irish widow who applied for charity at all establishments,

> as if saying 'Behold I am sinking, bare of help: ye must help me! I am your sister. . . .' They answer, 'No, impossible, thou art no sister of ours.'. . . She sank down in typhus-fever; died and infested her Lane with fever, so that 'seventeen other persons' died of fever there in consequence. . . . She proves her sisterhood; her typhus-fever kills *them*.[5]

So, by innumerable such 'organic filaments' is demonstrated the solidarity of mankind. And so does Dickens replicate this Carlylean Irish-widow paradigm in the typhus fever of Jo in *Bleak House*. Jo with his sickness is a ganglion connecting most — I think — of the organic filaments of all the almost innumerable characters in *Bleak House*. Man's sociality is demonstrated in the disaster which ensues when he negates the *Humanität* incumbent on him. Society is the concern of Thackerary's vast canvas, with his narrator omniscient, detached, ironic — the better to see and apprehend the various, shifting, multitudinous parts and whole of *Vanity Fair*. Trollope's great subject is man in his distinctively human institutions: Church, Parliament, Law, Finance, Marriage — 'The Way We Live Now' is considered with compelling sympathy from the myriad points of view of his myriad of interacting characters — and his sense of flux and multitudinousness is so keen that in his most characteristic novels he refuses closure, and characters move into ensuing chronicles. Balzac — who I believe is shown to have deployed *more characters* than any other novelist — creates the huge linking interactings of the great series of novels of *La Comédie Humaine* — not the comédie egotistique, metaphorique, biologique, or cosmologique, but *humaine*. Tolstoi takes up two aspects of distinctively *human* civilisation in 'War' and 'Peace'. Big subjects.

Hillis Miller moves towards defining the Victorian concern: 'In most Victorian novels, the protagonist comes to know himself and to fulfill himself by way of other people. Not "I think, therefore I am," but "I am related to others, therefore I am".[6] Hillis Miller goes on to explain how in Trollope's *Ayala's Angel*, for instance, Ayala is the more *existent* for each other person in the novel, in that each other person reveals as an aspect of Ayala and the action is reciprocal.

> In the same way, the source of meaning which makes language possible can be located in no single word, but only in the interaction of words in syntactical patterns. The power of structures of words to create meaning is usually taken for granted. It becomes visible in language turned back on itself, for example, in poetry (p. 136).

Poetry, he avers, is to language as the Victorian novel is to personal relationships.

I don't think it can be objected that novels of other periods are the same in this. The enormous length of Richardson's *Pamela* and *Clarissa* contrasts with the wonderful narrowness of their scope. The expansive 'humanity' of Fielding is of that classical Johnsonian kind that discovers 'general' truths of human nature, while the Victorian insists on historical change and specific truths. Smollett has many varied characters but works in episodes rather than a societal figuration. Sterne is Romantic in sentiment, Bloomsburian in method. Jane Austen flaunts and exploits her narrowness of scope. Scott, for all his glory, gives us costume-history.

Middlemarch may be the best illustration of the Victorianism of the Victorian novel. In its panorama of society we see man functioning and interacting in his conventions or institutions — church (and chapel), land-holding and inheritance, marriage, medicine, scholarship, politics, and labour. Provincial society exhibits the linkages better because there *are* more linkages there than in the more separate multitudinous lives in great cities. All the people of the town are aware of each other: Bulstrode's downfall *matters* here, where it would not so much in London. The coincidences in *Middlemarch* — Ladislaw happens to be connected both with Casaubon and with Bulstrode, and Dorothea happens on Ladislaw just when he is holding Rosamond's hands — these may mar the art of the novel, but they bear out George Eliot's concern with linkages, 'the stealthy convergence of human lots',[7] as she puts it, or the 'weavings and interweavings' of 'this particular web' (15: 105). Her putting her events forty years back also enables the better display of linkages of people to each other and to political events. *We* know when we read *Middlemarch* that the Reform Bill was ultimately passed. The relationships of Brooke and Ladislaw and Dorothea and the rest reveal George Eliot's idea of how it came to be passed, and sanctions, as it were, her characters' political visions.

Masses of details in *Middlemarch* serve to bear out the historicist-epistemological concern. Take the mere fact that Will Ladislaw went to Rugby — it is mentioned twice (9: 59, 60: 441). He couldn't have actually been there when Thomas Arnold was, but I think George Eliot permits herself an anachronism here because the Rugby ideal helps to define Ladislaw. Thomas Arnold was one of the first to learn and use German; a great admirer of Vico, he recognises Vico's humane historicist view in Herder and appropriates it in his teaching and in adapting Niebuhr's method in his own history of Rome. Even Mr Brooke seems to have 'gone into' Vico: he knew that 'history moves in circles' (2: 12). The kind of vocation to the public good which Ladislaw and Dorothea eventually answer to was a thing inculcated and quite standard at Rugby. Ladislaw in his continental aspect epitomises elements of the new German learning. Casaubon complains of him 'And now he wants to go abroad again, without any special object, save the vague purpose of what he calls culture, preparation for he knows not what' (9: 59). Wilhelm von Humboldt deliberately shaped his career in the interests of *Bildung*, devoting himself for some years to developing many sides of his human self — in science, art, music, history, philology, and eventually turning to an effective career in shaping German society, in education and politics. Similarly, Ladislaw's interests and capacities are notably *developed* — in painting, music, literature, *and* politics — the ultimate engagement. It is Ladislaw who indicates the provincialism and Philistinism of the English: Casaubon's work is utterly negligible, 'as so much English scholarship is, for want of knowing what is being done by the rest of the world (21: 154). . . . New discoveries are constantly making new points of view' (22: 164). Casaubon doesn't even *know* German, and the irony is that in Germany, with the new philology, comparative anthropology, comparative religion, they were really finding something like 'the Key to All Mythologies'.[8]

Man as distinguished from animals, is a *motiv* that runs through *Middlemarch*. Even Sir James Chettam, who is so amiably anti-culture, is affectionately distinguished from the animals and from primitive man who regards a mate as prey (6: 45). George Eliot implies the German definition of man as the distinctively linguistic animal; the theory of language as metaphor at base, of language and metaphor as making religion possible, of religion not as the superstition Comte considered it, but as notably expressivist in that man makes himself by it. These concepts develop from Vico through Hamann, and Herder, and come to English through Carlyle and Arnold, and are represented in Oxford by Max Müller and his writings on *The Science of Language* (1861, 1863) and *Introduction to The Science of Religion* (1872); and indeed they go on developing in German and English philosophy. Man looks before and after and makes himself and his worlds, or plots, with words. 'The right word', says George Eliot casually in *Middlemarch*, 'is always a power, and communicates its definiteness to our action' (31: 223). The word classifies, supplies 'This power of generalising which gives men so much the superiority in mistake over the dumb animals' (58: 432). It can be man's tragedy as well as his glory, contributing to the victimisation of Lydgate: 'Lydgate was bowing his neck under the yoke like a creature who had talons, but who had Reason too, which often reduces us to meekness' (58: 435). Dorothea and Mr Farebrother speculate on the sociality of insects, who 'for aught we know may hold reformed parliaments' (80: 575); but the effect of this is to insist on the culmination of man's language in government, in what Carlyle called 'Palaver House'.

George Eliot epistemoligises; she tries to imagine man without memory: 'Even without memory, the life is bound into one by a zone of dependence in growth and decay' (61: 450) — this almost unimaginable being suggests how memory is essentially human. We *are* our pasts, as Bulstrode has to learn. She boldly suggests our dependence on metaphor: 'we all of us, grave or light, get our thoughts entangled in metaphors, and act fatally on the strength of them' (10: 63). There is even an anticipation of our modern theory of fictions — which developed out of the *Bildung* idea through Nietzsche and Vaihinger. Here is Lydgate's ideal of the scientific process: the imagination in

the exercise of disciplined power — combining and constructing with the clearest eye for probabilities and the fullest obedience to knowledge; and then, in a yet more energetic alliance with *impartial* Nature, standing aloof to invent tests by which to try its own work.... Lydgate was enamoured of that ardous *invention* which is the very eye of research, provisionally framing its object and correcting it to more and more exactness of relation... (16: 122, my italics)

This vision of scientific method is also a vision of artistic method. And the invented fictions of novels are part of the dialectic of *Entwicklung*, man inventing himself in society by language, symbol, science, and art, and perpetually revising, in the words of Goethe which form an epigraph to Chapter 81, *Zum höchsten Dasein immerfort zu streben* — constantly striving towards the highest degree of existence. This is a culmination of the ideal of *Bildung*, which is never complete because human potential is infinite. This is George Eliot's vision of the future, her millenarianism as it has been called, more German at last I think than

Comtean. Arnold connected this German ideal with New Testament rhetoric, of 'having life more abundantly'. Dorothea develops out of the restrictions of her youth into a more abundant life, which will enrich the future.

NOTES

1 Michael Timko, 'The Victorianism of Victorian Literature', *New Literary History*, 6 (Spring, 1975) 607–22.
2 First published 1849; *Poems*, ed. Kenneth Allott (London: Longmans, 1965), p. 54.
3 Timko quotes from Carlyle's *Characteristics*.
4 Johann Gottfried von Herder, *Ideen zur Philosophie der Geschichte der Menschheit* (Leipzig, 1784). Translated as *Outlines of a Philosophy of the History of Man* by T. Churchill (London, 1800), p. 123.
5 T. Carlyle, *Past and Present*, III, ii, 'The Gospel of Mammonism'.
6 Hillis Miller, *The Form of Victorian Fiction* (Notre Dame and London: University of Notre Dame Press, 1968), p. 5.
7 *Middlemarch*, ed. G. S. Haight (Boston: Houghton Mifflin, 1956), 11:70.
8 W.J. Harvey indentifies Casaubon's subject as the tired old eighteenth-century idea that all pagan myth is corruption and diversification of the Genesis narrative. 'The Intellectual Background of the Novel: Casaubon and Lydgate', *Middlemarch: Critical Approaches to The Novel* (University of London: Athlone Press, 1967), pp. 25–37.

5 'Stealthy Convergence' in *Middlemarch*

ROBERT B. HEILMAN

'Stealthy convergence', it need hardly be said, is extracted from a longer phrase in *Middlemarch*: 'the stealthy convergence of human lots' (11: 70).[1] It is George Eliot's compact description of an ironic development of interconnection among people who do not expect it. It is in effect a restatement of 'No man is an island'. Yet its emphasis is different: less on the denial of separateness than on the almost imperceptible, or unperceived, process by which apparently independent lots turn out to be related. The primary process takes place, obviously, in the human experience depicted. But there is also a secondary process that is worth attention: it is an important ingredient in Eliot's depicting methods — her ways of bringing parts into coalescence and ultimate oneness. 'Convergence' then not only denotes a conceptual position but is a metaphor for artistic ordering. For Eliot's characters 'stealthy' means a near invisibility of the developments that tie their lives together. For Eliot's readers it images the inconspicuous devices by which the artist draws us from area to area — the local transitions as well as the organic fusions.

The oldest and simplest tie that binds is the chronological, the transition effected by the ticking of the clock. A temporal sequence seems to the human mind to have an inherent oneness. *Middlemarch* is chronological in traditional ways. After Dorothea says 'yes' to Casaubon, all that happens comes to us as it happens in time. Eliot gives no ground for another essay on how artists two-time time. (One may remark, in passing, that it is time for critics to untime themselves; time-talk must have a stop, for all its early paradoxes have aged into banalities.) Eliot's few variations from time-order are as old as epic practice — flashbacks and inset narratives. One flashback catches our eye because it is very subtly

47

tied in. Eliot climaxes her long initial portrait of Lydgate (Ch. 15) by recounting an earlier episode in his life. Here she shifts remarkably from her usual full specification to 'stealthy convergence', which at this point is a symbolic connection between past and present that remains unstated. As a medical student in Paris Lydgate had tried to marry an actress who, he was to discover, had coolly murdered her actor-husband during a stage scene in which her stabbing him could seem an accident. Overtly, Eliot says only that his proposal was due to Lydgate's 'impetuous folly' (p. 112). What she does not specify is the deeper symbolic tie between Lydgate's youthful proposal and his actual marriage, that is, his virtually suicidal attraction to beautiful, ruthless, even destructive women. Laure would reappear as Rosamond Vincy. (This use of the Laure story remarkably anticipates the Conrad technique of the 'pilot episode', just as the interpretation of a medical type remarkably anticipates what Somerset Maugham and Sinclair Lewis would see in doctors whom they portrayed.)

But in a multiplicity novel with as many strands of action as *Middlemarch* has, the problems of relationship are less temporal than spatial. How make ties among parallel strands? Actionally, of course, the parallel lines alter to convergent lines: as characters fall into unexpected relationships, the plots gradually blend in a massive dramatic movement that includes all participants, major and minor—Dorothea and Ladislaw, Lydgate and Rosamond, Vincys, Bulstrodes, Garths, Featherstone, Raffles. Perhaps no other novel so well symbolises, by its merging streams of narrative, the inevitability of linkages that forge an unanticipated community within, and involving much of, the literal community of Middlemarch.

My subject, however, is not the familiar one of unity from multiplicity, but the bridges between parallel lines, and the techniques of convergence. Cumbersome as she can be at times, Eliot never falls, if my observation is sound, into the old mechanics of grossly derricking the reader from Action A to Action B, as in this old standby: 'Let us now leave Esther seated in the park and renew our acquaintance with Coldfield in his cell'. Instead of such bald shifts there are various ingenuities of transition. One of these is an innovative employment of a technique that would become, much later, a standard feature of another art. It is significant enough to justify describing one example in some detail.

Dorothea Brooke dominates the first nine and a half chapters as she progresses to the altar with Casaubon; observers' comments on this affair introduce us indirectly to six supporting characters. Then Lydgate dominates the next eight and a half chapters, which also identify people important in his later life. From the Casaubons to Lydgate looks like a big shift in focus. Yet Eliot does not crudely drop the honeymooners, saying, 'We will now take a look at the stay-at-homes'. Rather she sneaks us across an invisible borderline between the newly-weds and others so smoothly that we hardly notice the process. Chapter 10 describes a big dinner just before the wedding. This is the right occasion for Eliot to use more intensely her method of having friends and neighbours discuss the principals: in doing this, the townspeople portray Dorothea and Casaubon further, introduce and sketch themselves, and reflect community tone. We are given almost a tape-recording of random party chatter, but beneath the air of randomness a controlled process directs our attention. Some speakers compare Dorothea with Rosamond Vincy; others, noting Casaubon's unrobust look, talk of illness and thus naturally allude to the town's new physician, Lydgate. Then it is Lydgate who opens Chapter 11, and he thinks about a subject continued from the party discussion: the difference between Rosamond and Dorothea. From this Eliot slips easily into portrayals of Rosamond and the other Vincys, including Fred Vincy and hence his girl, Mary Garth; and so on, until we have met Mary, Featherstone and his household, Bulstrode, and the hospital problems that involve Bulstrode, Lydgate, and Fare-brother. These details may be tedious, but we need them if we are to see clearly how Eliot, without palpable break or rude leap from one topic to another, has taken us adroitly, imperceptibly, from one love-affair to the makings of two different ones and to the supporting casts of some size. We have been gliding along a continuum of segments of a community-in-action, segments as of now independent or loosely connected, but appearing serially for one initial inspection as if they were panels of a polyptych.

This comparison suggests a series of separate but related 'stills', to use the photographic term. One goes in a natural, non-spasmodic, arranged route from one display to the contiguous display in a gallery, that is, from fictional object to object. They have been juxtaposed; the curator — in our case the novelist — has skilfully put side by side the actors, commentators, themes so that the observer goes naturally from phase to phase of an ordered exhibit. This description, however, is only partly accurate. We must not rest in a sense of stills and static displays, of elements that we make stops in front of. Instead we must attend to the narrative movement, the movement that I have called gliding and graceful, the artist's moving line of sight that we follow. Of course, there it is: moving pictures. Long before it emerged as a standard device, Eliot was using a cinematic technique. It was 'panning', that is, proceeding panoramically from one to another of the neighbouring components of groups or scenes. Let me return to Chapter 10 to note more precisely a detail of the camera work. We first see the engaged couple enter the drawing room; we move to the observers who talk about the couple, and then from these talkers to other men and women whom they talk about; then we follow those talked about — especially Rosamond and Lydgate, he thinking about her — into their lives beyond the party. No other nineteenth-century novelist, as far as I have observed, has hit upon this polished way of transferring us, if not insensibly at least without our feeling the graceless yank of an author's derrick, from part to part. (The comparison with cinema is purely to define, not to praise. We are too much given to lauding a predecessor for pioneering a style, method, or attitude that we think especially characteristic of our later time. Eliot's virtue is not to have anticipated a modern film technique, but to have hit on an admirable device which we can best identify as like a movie method.) Well, throughout *Middlemarch* Eliot often proceeds by topographic proximity, but I forego inventory of such transitions to observe some comparable aspects of her art.

Planning depends upon the artist's ability to see as neighbours, or bring together as neighbours, the elements that permit a visual cross-over. The invited cross-over is also a way of leading into meaning, for Eliot has a strong sense of parallels, analogies, and thematic variations. With or without physical juxtaposition, there is frequent psychological or moral juxtaposition. Eliot's sensibility tends towards next-door or side-by-side relationships, be they parallels with differences, or differences with parallels. She pans, so to speak, among ideas or meanings. Early on we see that Dorothea is a creature of ideals, but then we learn that the tough Rosamond has an ideal too, and that Lydgate seems to embody it (12: 88). Lydgate, in turn, has an ideal of medical practice. Eliot's caption for Book II, 'Old and Young', seems commonplace.

The theme is indeed an ancient one — egotism, power, and will in conflict with hopes, dreams, and ambitions — but it gains freshness through Eliot's juxtaposition of three variants among which she pans. Dorothea hopes to serve an old husband, but he is too self-enclosed to be open to help. Fred Vincy hopes to be served by a legacy from old Featherstone, who can therefore sadistically push Fred around. Lydgate hopes to serve the community in old Bulstrode's hospital, and so he is pressured by Bulstrode's self-righteousness and rigid evangelicalism.

Now, just when Lydgate caves in to Bulstrode on the hospital chaplaincy (Ch. 18), Eliot suddenly picks up the Casaubons (Ch. 19), whom we left as they took off on a honeymoon in Rome (Ch. 10). At first this shift may look like the rude puppeteering of a novelist falling back on an arbitrary transition. Yet we really have, not a gauche leap, but a juxtaposing of complementary narratives on the same theme — two eager idealists feeling educative blows by unanticipated crude reality, one in professional, the other in domestic, life. Eliot is panning thematically. She does this very ingeniously in a relationship hinted at by the rubric of Book v, 'The Dead Hand'. This phrase clearly applies to two similar cases but serves most effectively in tying in with them a third action that is superficially dissimilar. There are two literal 'dead hands', that is, wills through which dead men seek power over the living. Eliot treats ironically the testamentary ploys of Casaubon and Featherstone, whose plans are not carried out by history. But in Eliot's profoundest irony, their reversals are reversed by the reversal of Bulstrode. Just as the dead hand of the past cannot will the future for others, so one's own present, and hence future, cannot will one's own past dead. As Eliot put it, 'a man's past is not simply a dead history'. In the subtlest of the 'dead hand' variants, Bulstrode wants to rule his own past dead; he can try to kill it by letting Raffles die, but this leads only to new disasters that are, in Eliot's words, the 'second life [of] Bulstrode's past' (61: 450). This dead hand does rule on.

Eliot's putting things side by side in literal or metaphorical space — be it a preliminary to or an aspect of the 'stealthy convergence' in both human histories and her rendering of them — reflects a deep strain in her sensibility. It appears, finally, in her modal inclusiveness. *Middlemarch* achieves, as far as my knowledge goes, a fuller convergence of fictional modes than any other work of the century. Two unlike modes that emerge from the eighteenth century — the novel of manners and the Gothic novel — both appear in *Middlemarch*: one in the wit of the author and of Mrs Cadwallader, in the amusing dialogue and the recording of social styles; the Gothic in the mystery and ominousness of the Raffles episode and the secret history which it encloses. In its persistent play of ideas, the novel is philosophical; yet it also encompasses some wonderful farce, as on the occasion of Brooke's sherry-built campaign speech. It has strong elements of the grotesque: the 'expectations' theme, embodied in the hopeful heirs hanging around Featherstone, might be a fresh version of the unseemly Pockets surrounding grotesque Miss Havisham in *Great Expectations*. Then there is Eliot's dominant manner — the realism which we often think of casually as a historical displacement of these other modes. The diversity of modes does not mean incoherence; the modes converge into one unified history of a community, the disparateness of its components represented in part by the tonal variety.

There is an analogous convergence of stylistic modes: the frequent abstractions of Eliot's analytical and meditative passages joining with the richness of diverse sensory images by which she gives a concrete reality to scenes and people. Or she can merge conceptual opposites in the vitality of epigram or paradox. One excellent example is this: 'Marriage . . . had not yet freed' Dorothea from her 'oppressive liberty' (28: 202). Being 'freed' from 'liberty', and 'liberty' as 'oppressive' — a remarkable convergence of apparent contradictions in a very fine insight (one with especial applicability in our own day).

The convergence of modal and stylistic opposites in Eliot's technique is comparable to what happens in the marriages she portrays. Lydgate, the idealistic would-be scientific benefactor of mankind, marries a self-indulgent, whim-of-iron materialist. Fred Vincy, a leaner without much direction, marries sturdy, sensible, well-organised Mary Garth. But the most interesting marriage is that of Dorothea and Ladislaw, which, as Professor Haight observed long ago, is a convergence of the moral and the aesthetic. In this union, which I find much more expectable and probable than some readers do, there may be a faint allegorical touch of cultural history. Romantic as she is in various ways (she even imagines a Pantisocracy or Brook Farm [55: 401]), Dorothea has a strong Victorian cast: her sense of duty, her needing to serve, her wanting to quell selfishness, her accepting the importance of being earnest. Ladislaw, on the other hand, is pure Romantic, whether by formal design or by not quite conscious thrusts of the creative imagination. He is the outsider, the man without ties, the possessor of an acute sense of honour. His mother eloped with a Polish refugee-musician, the son of a political radical (one thinks of the Lensky–Skrebensky presence in Lawrence's *Rainbow*). He says to Dorothea, 'You see I come of rebellious blood on both sides' (37: 269). He seems a 'kind of Shelley' (37: 263) to Mr Brooke, who later modifies his view and sees Will, now his editor and political aide, as 'a sort of Burke with a leaven of Shelley' (51: 366) — a one-liner convergence of the twain. Meanwhile, Mrs Cadwallader has called him 'A sort of Byronic hero — an amorous conspirator' (38: 278). To describe Dorothea's voice Ladislaw twice uses that famous Romantic image, the 'Aeolian harp' (9: 59; 21: 155). Eliot herself gives a romantic picture of Will singing: 'he looked like an incarnation of the spring whose spirit filled the air — a bright creature abundant in uncertain promises' (47: 345). This acts as a riposte to lawyer Hawley's unromantic view of the entirely certain promise in the romantic young man: 'He'll begin with flourishing about the Rights of Man and end with murdering a wench. That's the style' (37: 262). Rights of Man, Shelley, Byron, Aeolian harp, spring song, a heritage exotic, rebellious and radical — may not these reveal, in Eliot's imagination, an unarticulated sense of Will as Romantic (with an upper-case *R* imposed on a lower-case *r*)? And hence a historical complement, as well as a moral one, for Dorothea as an embodiment of the Zeitgeist felt by the novelist? And further, the author's prescription for herself, whom, with great detachment, she partly embodies in Dorothea?

Such teasing speculations merely sketch a possible addition to the many instances of that convergence which in *Middlemarch* governs both substance and actional design. My business is less interpretation than exploration of the equivalence of the what and the how: what is experienced by the actors (the stealthy convergence of lots) imitated by how the audience experiences the actors in roles that will converge. The actors slide unperceivingly into relations unforeseen: the audience slides unawares from a focus on one apparently independent actor to another close by. This anticipation of cinematic panning requires proximity, but in *Middlemarch* the proximity never seems arbitrary. Rather it is an inconspicuous symbol of a connectedness to be revealed. The person — or theme — near-by turns out to be a moral near relation. Such relatedness is, of course, the index of community, that interactive whole which accommodates, without dissipating it, the infinite variety of beings and existences. Eliot grasped this fusion of disparates as few have done since. She enacts her vision in her art, which moulds many into one: actions and scenes, attitudes and meanings of characters, and then even literary modes (manners and Gothic, philosophy and farce, grotesque and realistic) and styles (the abstract and the concrete, the straightforward and the paradoxical). Convergence has many dimensions — in content, in ways of seeing it, in ways of forming it and presenting it.

NOTES

1 Chapter numbers and page references are to the Riverside edition of *Middlemarch*, ed. Gordon S. Haight (Boston: Houghton Mifflin, 1956).

6 *Antique Gems* from *Romola* to *Daniel Deronda*

JOSEPH WIESENFARTH

We know from George Eliot's notes for *Adam Bede*[1] that, from the beginning of her career as a novelist, she was characteristically careful about introducing anything into her fiction that she did not thoroughly understand. In that novel, before dressing her characters in the fashion peculiar to the turn of the century, she read and took notes from Fairholt's *Costume in England*.[2] From hose to headgear Hetty Sorrel attempts to be a fashionable lady on a milkmaid's pay. She even manages to buy herself a pair of large earrings, which were all the rage in 1799;[3] so that when the novelist designed a moral motif related to jewelry she made sure, first of all, that she had the correct design for the earrings themselves.[4] When writing *Romola* Eliot took infinite pains to get similar details accurately transcribed before turning them into the patterns of fiction.

She learned from the Reverend Charles William King's *Antique Gems: Their Origin, Uses, and Value as Interpreters of Ancient History*[5] that one expression of the Renaissance passion for antiquity was the collector's passion for ancient precious stones. Such gems were especially valuable if they were carved as intaglios (in which a figure is incised beneath the surface of the gem) or cameos (in which the gem is engraved in relief so that the raised design is one colour and the background another). Tito Melema, who has 'lustrous agate-like eyes' (67: ii, 392)[6] tells Nello that he has 'intaglios and cameos, both curious and beautiful' which he wants to sell (3: i, 58). Such stones were bought in the fifteenth century for their monetary as well as for their mystic value as healing agents.

While the monetary value of gems is completely intelligible to us — for good gems are as rare and costly as ever — it is interesting to note the relative value of the ruby, the emerald, the diamond, and the sapphire in Renaissance Italy. According to Cellini's *Orificeria* (1560), the diamond was worth ten times the price of the sapphire, the emerald four times the price of the diamond, and the ruby twice the price of the emerald, eight times the price of the diamond, and eighty times the price of the sapphire (*Notebook*, p. 79).

The mystic value of gems is much less intelligible to us today. King devotes eighty pages of *Antique Gems* to explaining it to his readers. But the mystic value of gems is more readily and briefly explained by John Ayrton Paris in his *Pharmacologia*, which George Eliot used in the writing of *Felix Holt* and *Middlemarch*.[7] When the cause of illness of any kind was a mystery to man, he attributed it to malignant spirits. Gems were considered to be the 'residence of spirits'. 'Such substances, from their beauty, splendour, and value', Paris reports, were thought

> well adapted as receptacles for good spirits.... The precious stones were, at first, only used as amulets or external charms, but, like many other articles of the Materia Medica, they passed, by a mistake in the mode of their application, from the outside to the inside of the body, and they were accordingly powdered and administered as specifics (*Notebook*, p. 60).

In *Romola*, Bernardo Rucellai, a wealthy collector who is interested in the rarest stones money can buy, purchases Tito's most exquisite gems. Bernardo Scala buys only those gems that he thinks will be medicinally effective against the gout. Rucellai and Scala thus become examples of the opulence and superstition of Renaissance Italy. The Medicean collection of antique gems that the invading French buy and the prophylactic rings that Bardo de' Bardi wears by prescription amplify these same characteristics of Florence.

None of the gems that Tito sells are in any way ordinary. Rucellai buys 'the chief rings' in Melema's collection — one of them 'is a fine sard, engraved with a subject from Homer' (39: ii, 94). Sards, as King notes, are extremely hard and 'retain their original polish'; on them are 'found the finest works of the Greek artists' (*Notebook*, p. 78). Scala buys two rare stones: an agate with a *lusus naturae* in it and a Jew's stone. The design of the *lusus naturae* (the trick of nature) is 'Cupid riding on the lion' (7: I, 122)—the same subject that is engraved on the celebrated 'Emerald signet of Polycrates' and illustrated in *Antique Gems* (p. 316). The Jew's stone was valuable in itself and yet more valuable with an intaglio in it.[8]

(Reproduced from C.W. King, *Antique Gems, Their Origin, Uses, and Value as Interpreters of Ancient History; and as Illustrative of Ancient Art; with Hints to Gem Collectors* (London: John Murray, 1860)).

Tito's own ring, which he eventually sells to a Genoese, is also a remarkable gem: 'This is a curious and valuable ring, young man', says Domenico Cennini. 'This intaglio of the fish with the crested serpent above it, in the black stratum of the onyx, or rather nicolo, is well shown by the surrounding blue of the upper stratum' (4: I, 64). 'On this gem,' says King, 'fine Roman intagli occur more frequently than upon any other after the Sard' (*Antique Gems*, p. 11). The planetary figure carved in the nicolo is that of *Cetus*, 'a big fish with a bent tail and a wide mouth', and, King explains, 'if cut on a stone, with a large crested serpent with a long mane above it, it gives good luck at sea and restores lost things' (*Antique Gems*, p. 441).[9] Tito also has 'a fine Cleopatra cut in sardonyx' (3: I, 58), the subject suggesting its Egyptian origin during the time of Roman domination. King describes just such a stone in *Antique Gems*: 'a bust of Cleopatra, given in exact accordance with the prescribed type of the Queen, as seen on the oldest monuments, adorned with a profusion of small curls and many rows of necklaces, but worked out with extreme delicacy in the black layer of Onyx in very flat relief' (p. 116). When one looks closely at the gems Tito carries, it becomes evident that George Eliot took great care to provide him with choice items.

The effect of her precision on the novel is varied and subtle. The sale of the gems brings 'a man's ransom' (9: I, 148), and

Tito's refusal to pay that ransom is an indictment of his conduct. The gems also tell us something about Baldassarre, whom we generally see as a beggarly, mad, and vengeful old man. At one time, however, he must have been otherwise, for only a scholarly, masterful, and patient man could have put together such an extraordinary collection of gems.

Tito's own ring is also used to advantage in forwarding the novel's plot. Bratti notices it and takes Tito to Nello; at the barber's Melema is introduced to Domenico Cennini, who directs him to Bardo, Scala, and Rucellai. Among them he finds a wife and a fortune. Tito's ring is so distinctive that Fra Luca immediately recognises it, and Melema feels compelled to sell it to a merchant whom Baldassarre presently sees wearing it in Genoa and who tells him about Bratti's shop where the ring was purchased. Ironically, a ring that affirms the binding relationship of Tito to Baldassarre continues to link father to son in spite of Melema's attempt to break the tie by selling the symbol of it. The 'intaglio of the fish with crested serpent above it' nicely reinforces this point. Tito claims, as King indicated, that 'the stone and intaglio are of virtue to make the wearer fortunate, especially at sea, and also restore to him whatever he may have lost' (4: 1, 64). But Baldassarre, who was literally lost at sea, returns to Tito, who emphatically does not want him back at all. But the virtue of the ring proves too strong for Tito to circumvent it. This use of the ring in *Romola* develops into a striking illustration of how Eliot's doctrine of consequences works itself out in circular fashion beyond the intention of the wrongdoer.

Romola avoids such consequences by acts of selfless love. She redeems the necklace that Tito had given to Tessa as a sign of affection and returns it to the guileless girl. By seeking Tessa through Bratti, just as Baldassarre sought Tito through him, Eliot has Romola's forgiveness take the same path as Baldassarre's vengeance. Bernardo del Nero once told Bardo that Romola was 'a rare gem' that Tito did not truly value (5: 1, 113), and at no point in the novel is this more manifest than when the wronged wife returns her husband's pledge of love to his simple-minded mistress. Tito betrays both his father and his wife — one a collector of rare gems and the other a rare gem herself — because he chooses to act in the wily manner of the serpent carved in a coil as a ring within a ring. The jewelry motif in *Romola*, which began in George Eliot's mind as part of the realistic background of fifteenth-century Florence, gradually develops into a complex rendering of character, value and theme in the novel.

King's *Antique Gems* also served George Eliot in the composition of *Middlemarch* and *Daniel Deronda*. When Celia asks her sister to divide the jewelry left to them by their mother, in Chapter 1 of *Middlemarch*, Dorothea, after refusing to take any of the gems, suddenly changes her mind:

> She was opening some ring-boxes, which disclosed a fine emerald with diamonds, and just then the sun passing beyond a cloud sent a bright gleam over the table.
>
> 'How very beautiful these gems are!' said Dorothea, under a new current of feeling, as sudden as the gleam. 'It is strange how deeply colours seem to penetrate one, like scent. I suppose that is the reason why gems are used as spiritual emblems in the Revelation of St John. They look like fragments of heaven. I think that emerald is more beautiful than any of them'.[10]

In his discussion of 'Gems of the Apocalypse' King emphasises St John's discussion of the Smaragdus, 'by which', says King, 'he probably means to express the true Emerald' (*Antique Gems*, p. 429). The emerald is a peculiarly apt gem for Dorothea to treasure, because from antiquity it was believed to be a cure for myopia. Antiquity's greatest gossip, Pliny, tells us that Nero 'used to view the combats of gladiators in the arena through an Emerald, "Smaragdo spectabat"' (*Antique Gems*, p. 34). Dorothea, we recall, prefers her dog Monk to the puppy Sir James offers her because she knows that even though she is nearsighted she is not likely to trip over a St Bernard. Dorothea's spiritual vision is also myopic, as the epigraph to Chapter 2 indicates. She sees the helmet of Mambrino with Don Quixote instead of the barber's basin with Sancho Panza. She also sees Edward Casaubon as Augustine, Pascal, and Bossuet, not as Edward Casaubon. But emeralds, which as Pliny says, 'refresh the wearied eye' (*Antique Gems*, p. 35), seem also finally to refresh Dorothea's vision in *Middlemarch*; the pattern of events revealed in the quotation from Chapter 1, given above, is repeated in Chapter 83.

In Chapter 1 Dorothea resolves not to take any gems; the sunlight then suddenly strikes the emeralds; her feelings are quickened, and she takes what she thought she could not have. In

Chapter 83 Dorothea resolves not to marry Ladislaw; lightning then suddenly flashes, her passion is quickened, and she resolves to marry the man she thought she could not marry. In Chapter 1 a 'current of feeling' passes through Dorothea (1: 10); in Chapter 83 the current becomes 'the flood of her young passion' (83: 594). In the end Dorothea no longer needs an apocalyptic excuse to accept a man who, like the emeralds, is characteristically described in images of brightness.

Gems also figure in a significant sequence of events in *Daniel Deronda*, but their use in that novel is strikingly anticipated in her long poem *The Spanish Gypsy*. There Don Silva gives Fedalma a casket of jewels as a pledge of his love for her. They are, he says, 'precious signs / Of long transmitted honour, heightened still / By worthy wearing'.[11] Among these are rubies, which, as we saw, were considered in the Renaissance the most precious of gems. Dolfo Spini's outrage at Tito in *Romola*, therefore, is unbounded because Melema betrays Spini just after Dolfo has given him his best ruby as a seal of their confederacy. Spini's richest gift, however, has bought only the basest treachery. Fedalma's rubies signify something like treachery too. Silva's presentation of the jewels occurs within doors and alternates with the sounds of prisoners' chains out of doors in a scene that has the effect of montage in the poem. Among the prisoners is the Gypsy chieftain, Zarca, who proves to be Fedalma's father. A large gold necklace, 'most finely wrought' (*Gypsy*, Bk. i, 108), that he wore has been taken from him and added to the jewels Don Silva gives Fedalma. When father and daughter acknowledge each other, Zarca flings away her circlet of rubies and Fedalma immediately divests herself of all of Silva's gems: 'Now good gems we part', says she. 'Speak of me always tenderly to Silva' (*Gypsy*, Bk. i, p. 162). But the gold necklace which links child and father is kept and, eventually, after Zarca's death, is worn by Fedalma as her badge of succession to leadership of the Gypsy people.

In *Daniel Deronda* Gwendolen Harleth owns an Etruscan necklace set with turquoises that once belonged to her father. Like Tito Gwendolen is anxious to sell the gems that were a father's gift. She sells the necklace, but Deronda redeems it for her. On her wedding day Gwendolen receives a diamond necklace from her husband, which Grandcourt permits his former mistress, Lydia Glasher, to send her. The diamonds arrive with a note that poisons them: 'I am the grave in which your chance of happiness is buried as well as mine', writes Lydia.[12] Gwendolen becomes hysterical and collapses. From this point forward in the novel the diamonds become the touchstone of Grandcourt's mastery of his new wife: 'the cord which united her with this lover and which she had hitherto held by the hand, was now being flung over her neck' (31: 401–2). Gwendolen, who is at first presented as a masterly horsewoman, now, we are told, 'answered to the rein' (35: 482).[13] The irony is remarkably subtle when the significance of turquoise is remembered. '*Turquoise*,' says King, 'is useful for riders. As long as one wears it his horse will not tire, nor throw him. It is also good for the eyes and averts accidents' (*Antique Gems*, p. 427). Gwendolen, hysterical on her wedding day, would have done better to stick with her turquoise and avoided the Grandcourt diamonds altogether. This interpretation is reinforced when we remember that Gwendolen is likened to Creüsa, the slaughtered bride of the faithless Jason, whom Medea sends a poisoned gift on her wedding day.

Lydia Glasher, like Medea, is an exile without legal recourse. She has left her homeland and her husband for Grandcourt. Nine years having passed and four children having been born, he has not married her and seeks to cast her off for Gwendolen. The law is on Grandcourt's side in support of the intended moral injustice. Lydia's reaction to his demands is 'stifled fury'; her feeling for his children is 'savage glory'. Faithless to her promise not to marry Grandcourt, Gwendolen fears Mrs Glasher — 'the woman who had the poisoning skill of a sorceress' (44: 616). Lydia determines to act against Gwendolen on her wedding day, 'not knowing whether she had done her children harm' and refusing 'to give up a purpose which was a sweet morsel to her vindictiveness' (30: 397). Lydia sends the diamonds with the note that poisons them: 'Truly here were poisoned gems, and the poison had entered into this poor young creature'. Grandcourt finds his bride 'pallid, shrieking as it seemed with terror, the jewels scattered around her on the floor' (31: 407). Seeking mastery and revenge in the absence of justice, sacrificing the welfare of her children, acting the part of a sorceress with the moral poison of fear and guilt, recreating the irrationality of love turned to hate, Lydia Glasher is Medea. Legally right, morally wrong, poisoned on her wedding day, Gwendolen is Creüsa. Rich, callous, rational, powerful, and, in the end, drowned after being struck from his yacht by the boom of a sail, Grandcourt is Jason.[14]

The turquoises stand outside the vortex of this destructive classical myth into which the diamonds drag Gwendolen,[15] and they are associated with Deronda, who is linked to the pledge of salvation implicit in Israel's return from exile to the promised land. In *Daniel Deronda*, in short, Eliot's use of King's factual material leads her fiction into the world of mythic significance.

Charles William King's *Antique Gems* is only one of many books which George Eliot read and from which she took detailed notes for her novels. But it has a special place in the study of her canon — as such other popular scholarly works like Paris's *Pharmacologia* do — because she not only had constant recourse to it while composing her novels but also because it stimulated the growth and power of her imagination to such a degree that we can see George Eliot's fiction achieving symbolic significance and mythic dimension by way of the curious, particular, and ineluctable facts that King made so abundantly available to her.

NOTES

1   Joseph Wiesenfarth, 'George Eliot's Notes for *Adam Bede*', *Nineteenth-Century Fiction*, 32 (1977), 127–65.
2   Ibid., 154.
3   Ibid.
4   For a discussion of the distinction between Hetty and Dinah Morris suggested by the jewellry motif in *Adam Bede*, see Bonnie S. Zimmerman, '"Radiant as a Diamond": Jewelry and the Female Role', *Criticism*, 19 (1977), 212–22.
5   C[harles] W[illiam] King, *Antique Gems: Their Origin, Uses, and Value as Interpreters of Ancient History; and as Illustrative of Ancient Art; with Hints to Gem Collectors* (London: John Murray, 1860). George Eliot took copious notes from King's work and entered them into her Commonplace Notebook; see George Eliot, *A Writer's Notebook, 1854–1879*, ed. Joseph Wiesenfarth (Charlottesville, Va.: University Press of Virginia, 1981), pp. 75–82; hereafter cited as *Notebook*.
6   *Romola*, 2 vols (19 and 20) of *The Works of George Eliot*, Cabinet Edition, 24 vols (Edinburgh and London: William Blackwood and Sons, 1878–). As early as Ch. 4 Piero di Cosimo remarks that Tito's 'eyes' have an 'agate-like brightness and depth' (I, 63).
7   In addition to King's discussion of the 'Mystic Virtues' of gems (pp. 389–470) and 'Prophylactic rings' (p. 459), George Eliot gathered information on their medicinal use from John Aryton Paris's *Pharmacologia* (London: Samuel Highley, 9th edn. 1843) and copied it into her *Notebook*, p. 60.

8   The 'Jew's stones' were, in fact, 'Gnostic amulets ... [mistakenly] ascribed to the ancient Hebrews', *Antique Gems*, p. 370; see also *Notebook*, p. 194, n. 2.

9   A different interpretation is proposed by Felicia Bonaparte: 'The intaglio of a fish with a crested serpent above it on Tito's ring ... suggests Bacchus, the epiphanic god of the sea who numbers among his specific creatures the serpent' (*The Triptych and the Cross: The Central Myths of George Eliot's Poetic Imagination*, The Gotham Library [New York: New York University Press, 1979], p. 91).

10 George Eliot, *Middlemarch*, ed. Gordon S. Haight, Riverside Editions (Boston: Houghton Mifflin, 1956), p. 10; subsequent references are to this edition.

11 *The Works of George Eliot: The Spanish Gypsy*, Cabinet Edition (London and Edinburgh, n.d.), Bk. I, p. 102; subsequent references are to this edition.

12 *Daniel Deronda*, ed. Barbara Hardy (Harmondsworth: Penguin Books 1967), Ch. 31, p. 406.

13 On the jewelry motif in general in this novel see Albert R. Cirillo, 'Salvation in *Daniel Deronda*: The Fortunate Overthrow of Gwendolen Harleth', *Literary Monographs*, ed. Eric Rothstein and Thomas K. Dunseath (Madison, Milwaukee, London: University of Wisconsin Press, 1967), I, 201–44; esp. pp. 213–16.

14 For an extended discussion of the use of the Jason — Medea — Creüsa analogy in *Deronda*, see Joseph Wiesenfarth, *George Eliot's Mythmaking*, Reihe Siegen 1 (Heidelberg: Carl Winter, 1977), pp. 215–19.

15 In so far as the Grandcourt diamonds are called 'poisoned gems' it should be noted that King records the following: '*Diamond* has the virtue of resisting all poisons, yet if taken inwardly is itself a deadly poison.... It baffles magic arts, dispels vain fears, and gives success in law suits. It ... renders the wearer bold and virtuous' (*Antique Gems*, p. 419). George Eliot draws on this description but turns it around to use the diamonds against Gwendolen, who is poisoned by 'a sorceress' and turned into a weakling by a woman defrauded of her moral, if not her legal, rights.

7 The Choir Invisible: The Poetics of Humanist Piety

MARTHA S. VOGELER

To celebrate the centenary of George Eliot's death there is no more appropriate work in all her canon than the 45-line poem whose title is its first line: 'O May I Join the Choir Invisible'. The various George Eliot convocations this year are fulfilments of her wish to live again in minds made better by her presence. The poem also quite independently engages our larger literary and philosophic interests. To appreciate it fully we need to consider its inspiration, its analogues, its reception, and its usage; and we must bravely confront its textual difficulties. Much of this has never been done.[1] Moreover, the poem has virtually disappeared from anthologies of Victorian literature. Such neglect is intensely ironic for the same reason that our interest in the poem this year is so fitting: it teaches that immortality consists in the survival of influence.

In radically redefining a received Christian doctrine while implicitly affirming its seriousness in a cryptic kind of wisdom literature, George Eliot was indeed a Victorian sage. Her claim to this title rests, of course, on her novels; yet she once told her publisher that each of her poems contained an idea she cared about 'strongly' and wished to 'propagate'.[2] That 'The Choir Invisible' rests on secular rather than Christian presuppositions is evident from the outset, for her Latin epigraph is of Stoic origin. It comes from a letter of Cicero's conveying his anxiety about how best to perpetuate the memory of a beloved daughter. 'I am', he says, 'more concerned about the long ages, when I shall not be here, than about my short day.' In the preceding passage he vows

64

to 'consecrate her memory by every kind of memorial borrowed from the genius of all the masters, Greek and Latin'.[3] George Eliot was similarly eclectic in honouring George Henry Lewes's memory after his death. She arranged for Dr Thomas Sadler, a Unitarian minister known to the family, to conduct Lewes's funeral at Highgate Cemetery chapel, a decision her friend Herbert Spencer thought evidence of the 'compromising sentiment she sometimes displayed in such matters'; and she established a Studentship in Physiology at Cambridge in Lewes's name, believing that he would 'delight to live in a series of lives'.[4]

For herself, too, surviving in the thoughts of only family and friends was not enough. As her best assurance of immortality she looked to her future readers. Indeed, she once said, 'If I live five years longer, the positive result of my existence on the side of truth and goodness will outweigh the small negative good that would have consisted in my not doing anything to shock others' (*Letters*, ii, 342). Was ever moral calculus so pathetic? Or so correct? Of all her works, 'The Choir Invisible' has provided the most apt formulas for paying her homage. Conducting her funeral service at Highgate, as he had Lewes's two years before, Dr Sadler easily reconciled his own attenuated Christianity with her spiritualised humanism. He quite naturally quoted Christ's words and her poem to express his conviction of her surviving presence.[5] Several obituary notices quoted its second and third lines, and they were soon inscribed on her monument, close to Lewes's, in the unconsecrated portion of Highgate Cemetery.

Nearly seven years elapsed between her completion of 'The Choir Invisible' in August 1867 and its publication in *The Legend of Jubal and Other Poems* in 1874. To emphasise its significance she placed it at the end of the collection, as Tennyson would do with 'Crossing the Bar' and Browning with the Epilogue to 'Asolando' — other poems in which a moving anticipation of death is expressed in a characteristic mode of affirmation.[6] Yet there is truth in the judgement of her early biographer, Mathilde Blind, that her verse as a whole reveals 'the profound sadness of her view of life'.[7] Her earliest published poem, written in her youthful Evangelical phase (and, interestingly enough, on immortality), mingles sadness at losing the beauties of the natural world at death with a lyrical assertion that both the beloved Bible and kindred would be enjoyed again in heaven (Haight, p. 26). Unable to believe in such a promise when she wrote *The Spanish*

Gypsy, she could only compensate its heroine by giving her the gratification of duty fulfilled, tragic though the consequences are. Fedalma, rejecting selfish happiness in this world, cries, 'I will not take a heaven / Haunted by shrieks of far-off misery'. It was while working on this poem that George Eliot conceived of the metaphor of the Choir Invisible as a substitute for that lost heaven, an inspiration and reward for those who, like Fedalma, seek to assuage the world's 'shrieks of far-off misery'.

Of those who lack such altruism, and hence apparently fail to qualify for such immortality, nothing is said in 'The Choir Invisible'. Satan and hell, as well as God, are absent from the poem's eschatology; heaven, of a sort, alone remains. Ignoring as it does the causal connection between sin and suffering, and entertaining only that between goodness and bliss, 'The Choir Invisible' is radically unlike George Eliot's larger works. In it she was free from the constraints that her providential, moralistic sense of the world order normally imposed: here she could triumph over the actual, the disheartening, and celebrate the possible, the inspiring. But not without cost in credibility. There is nothing in the poem of the pain that joining the Choir Invisible inflicts on the living — pain of the sort George Eliot herself experienced during months of harrowing anguish after Lewes's death.

The transcendentalism of 'The Choir Invisible' is one reason for regarding it as an ode. Moreover, like other nineteenth-century odes, the poem treats an elevated theme of universal interest in one voice conveying strong emotion. And though it lacks the formal and substantive features of the classical ode, reverberations remain. The Pindaric ode's mythological components are suggested by George Eliot's own mythic construct, the Choir itself; its philosophic content by her teaching that virtue and nobility lead to joy; its celebration of some objective physical attain-units suggest the strophe, antistrophe, and epode. I will venture to units suggest the strophe, antistrophe and epode. I will venture to call them 'strophes' here to keep this view of the poem as an ode before us, and also because 'strophe' in contemporary usage is indeed applied to modern irregular stanzas.[8]

The first strophe states the central theme in its opening line of aspiration that sets the tone of high seriousness. The initial 'O', consciously spelt without the 'h', represents longing and not exclamation, promotes serenity rather than arousal, and saves the 'may' from being heard as a quite undesirable interrogative. It also links the poem to Christian hymns, so many of which begin in aspiration or supplication with one form or the other of 'O', the vowel anticipating the vowels of the terminal 'Amen'.

Like many hymns, 'The Choir Invisible' asserts that the dead shall in some manner live. Unlike Christian immortality — or, more strictly, the afterlife of the resurrected — this afterlife is attained through a saving relationship not with a deity but with men and women both living and dead. The redemptive scheme constitutes a cycle of temporal and transtemporal influence: the noble acts of the living and the dead — those in time and those beyond time — inspire the living, and the living, in their turn, die and inspire their still living counterparts; and so on. Reward for virtue lies not in seeing God but in joining in that work in the world — the ever more intense diffusion of good — that the Third Person of the Trinity, in traditional religious language, performed; sanctification. Because the amount of good the dead may do is boundless, the intensity of life they may attain is unlimited: they live wherever and whenever their influence for good is felt — and, we may assume, in proportion, for good is certainly relative. They are present in 'pulses stirred to generosity', in 'deeds of daring rectitude', in 'thoughts sublime'. Hence the existential increment enjoyed by the Choir Invisible encompasses the traditional triad of feeling, action, and thought — the whole of human life. The omnipresent Choir constitutes a secular version of the communion of saints; the fellowship of its holy spirits is poured out upon all who believe in them.

The second strophe, more than twice as long as the first and the last, catalogues the functions performed by the Choir Invisible. The abstract language is not altogether intelligible, even with the poet's own partial exegesis. Writing to Charles Ritter, the French translator of the poem, George Eliot explained that 'breathing as beauteous order' stood in apposition to making 'undying music in the world'. Music, she affirmed, '*is* order in tones'. The 'presence of the spirit' is felt 'in' and 'by' the 'beauteous order which it helps to create'. (To this account she might have added the root meaning of 'inspiration', so often drawn upon by Romantic poets for their imagery.) By breathing-in the regenerating spirit, the 'beauteous order' controls 'with growing sway' the 'growing life of man' (*Letters*, vii, 56). Here we are re-

minded of the 'beauteous forms' that in 'Tintern Abbey' Wordsworth makes the source of moral, aesthetic, and visionary
experience.

George Eliot's conception of 'the growing life of man' expresses
the pervasive mid-Victorian belief in a kind of holistic moral evolution, for which she elsewhere employed the term 'meliorism'. U.
C. Knoepflmacher has compared her idea of an evolving culture
to Goethe's and to Matthew Arnold's, and suggests that culture
for her as for Arnold embodied the 'essence of Christianity'.[9]
That, of course, is the English phrase she used to translate the
title of the work by Ludwig Feuerbach that helped to convert her
from Christian Evangelicalism to relgious humanism, *Das Wesen
des Christenthums*. By reducing theology to anthropology, Feuerbach sought to show that religious conceptions are projections of
the mind, and, specifically, that belief in immortality is man's
attempt to satisfy a human wish by attributing to the individual
what belongs only to the race.[10] Even before she translated
Feuerbach, George Eliot had planned a study of the idea of a
future life that was announced as forthcoming along with *The
Essence of Christianity*. It never materialised; but can we not see
'The Choir Invisible' as a belated and distilled substitute for it? In
her poem, immortality is indeed a projection of the mind in so far
as it exists only in memory and vision, an attribute of the race in
so far as it is a universal social inheritance and a faculty of man's
moral evolution.

Though 'The Choir Invisible' assumes man's capacity for sympathy and, for the most part, neglects his darker traits and deeds,
the poem advocates no indiscriminate reverence for humanity.
George Eliot apotheosises not man but only his best qualities — which for Feuerbach constituted the essence of Christianity.
In her second strophe she equates joining the Choir Invisible with
inheriting 'that sweet purity / For which we struggled'. Purity is
sweet to the dead because in life they so long sought it despair-
ingly and in vain. To Ritter she explained that the diction of the
passage that speaks of the 'widening retrospect that bred despair'
was 'precise', and she declared that she had written out of her
own experience. 'Life is necessarily a widening prospect as we
look back upon it', and 'to many ... it is a retrospect of broken
resolutions which make each succeeding resolution less hopeful,
and in this way breed "despair"'. Her novels, of course, chart
such melancholy vistas for many of their characters.

In the second strophe's three lines on the 'rebellious flesh' there is something of the same ambiguity that William Empson complained of in Wordsworth's 'Tintern Abbey'. Empson blamed Wordsworth's 'loose rhetoric' and intellectual 'shuffling' on his 'attempt to be uplifting yet non-denominational, to put across as much pantheism as would not shock his readers'.[11] George Eliot's analogous obscurity lies in the lines characterising what it is in man's life that 'breeds despair'. Terming the flesh 'rebellious' without naming the authority against which it rebels, she seems to equate the flesh with the 'vicious parent' said to shame what it has spawned, 'anxious penitence'. Yet surely she could not wish to reduce all immorality to sensuality. That it is the flesh which is 'quick-dissolved' in death seems clear because she told Ritter that 'dissolved' had 'no such fixed narrowed associations in English as in French'; Hamlet, she noted, 'even used the word "melt" without exciting ridicule or offence in this connection'.

We seem on firmer ground, surprisingly, when the poem's imagery shifts from the physiological to the musical, from man's negative to his positive record. The 'discords' of the flesh are said to be 'quenched by meeting harmonies'. Is this not because death brings transcendence over all immorality as well as over the flesh with which it is associated? If so, George Eliot is asserting as reality what the Latin proverb merely enjoins: *de mortuis nil nisi bonum* — of the dead speak only good. In her poem, only the good remains to be spoken of after death. A mysterious winnowing process, parallel to Christianity's forgiveness of sins, occurs in air that is therefore rightly called 'large and charitable'.

And the dead self is inevitably the remembered essence of the 'rarer, better, truer self' that 'sobbed religiously in yearning song' and aspired to ease the world's burdens. That earthly song is 'religious' because of its moral motivation; the music of the Choir Invisible is 'religious' because of its moral consequences. In life the better self accepts necessity but yearns for what can 'yet be better', eventually transforming itself into the 'divinely human' image that exists potentially within. Mankind's old gods are thus replaced by its own exalted humanity. The conception forcibly reminds us of the de-mythologised Christ figure that George Eliot found so attractive in Charles Hennell's *Inquiry Concerning the Origin of Christianity*, which eroded her orthodoxy, in Strauss' *Das Leben Jesu*, which she translated, in Renan's *La Vie de Jésus*, which she defended, and in other contemporary works, notably Seeley's *Ecce Homo*.

Human perfectibility sanctified as religion is also a theme of the poetry she valued. *In Memoriam*, she judged, 'enshrines the highest tendency of this age'. Michael Wolff has pointed out that in one passage Tennyson adopts a supplicating stance remarkably similar to hers:[12]

> Let knowledge grow from more to more,
> But more of reverence in us dwell;
> That mind and soul, according well,
> May make one music as before,
>
> But vaster. . . .

In both poems the spatial adjective 'vaster' registers in counter-point to the temporal idea of immortality, the poet's central concern. An article of faith in both poems, too, is that the wisdom of the race is cumulative. The idea fascinated and encouraged many other nineteenth-century writers. It appears conspicuously in Shelley's poetry, for example. And is not Pater's 'Gioconda' the embodiment of such accrued experience? And Arnold's Culture? And Carlyle's Heroes? And Huxley's Science?

Whether secular imagery could do full justice to George Eliot's theme is an interesting question raised by the later lines of the second strophe. There, in exalting the 'rarer, better, truer self', she falls back upon the emotive and associative richness that only Christian diction could provide. The Eucharist seems to be suggested by the image clusters of a 'sanctuary' (the chancel and altar), of a shaping 'forth before the multitude' and 'raising worship' to 'higher reverence' (the public elevation and adoration of the elements), 'mixed with love' (the wine and water); while in the midst of these phrases the words 'divinely human' characterise the mystery the sacrament celebrates. Moreover, the Apocalypse seems to lie behind the cosmic imagery with which the strophe concludes. Even the Choir Invisble, it suggests, is not, after all, eternal: it lives only so long as the race and its world—'human time' and the 'human sky'—prevail. The metaphor of a scroll 'unread forever' must have been particularly painful for a writer!

The third strophe offers a secular counterpart to another Christian theme, salvation through Christ. 'Life to come' is made more glorious by those who have attained it; by emulating them we enter into their glory, as the Christian enters into the glory of Christ by emulating him. The passage reminds us that George

Eliot shared the curiously intense admiration of many Victorians, including some secularists, for the *Imitation of Christ,* the fifteenth-century devotional work that teaches the re-enactment of Christ's self-renunciation (Haight, pp. 18, 66, 95). In the next passage she brings herself as the poet back into our consciousness by using the first person pronoun, not heard since its use in the opening line. Unlike Keats, who declares in his ode that he will fly to the nightingale on the viewless wings of poesy, and then finds himself already with the bird, his symbol for the immortality of art, she can only pray that she may 'reach that purest heaven' so that in her translated state she may proffer the cup of strength to those in 'some great agony'. But even in this tentative form, the projection of her imagination prepares us for the apotheosis of death with which the poem ends. Like Keats' unseen nightingale, the invisible choir has been heard, and it has made the poet half in love with easeful death because in death one may enjoy a more intense diffusion of good than is possible in life. Though Keats eventually recognises the tragic gulf between the immortal bird and himself amidst the hungry generations that sit and hear men groan, George Eliot proclaims a permanent triumph over both death and sorrow: the music of the Choir Invisible is 'the gladness of the world'.

For George Eliot, we know, music was a source of personal delight so intense that it became part of her sacramental view of human experience. From music she drew metaphors for the human sympathy that binds man to man, the living to the dead. An 'invisible choir of all the dead' even figures in *The Spanish Gypsy* as a simile for the solemn sound of a bell tolling for the departed — those who have attained the 'more diffusive life'. And Fedalma elsewhere hears music that awakens her anew to 'life in unison with a multitude'.[13] Though Fedalma's identification is with the living, George Eliot believed that music could open a door to the transcendent. It was, she once insisted, an art superior to painting and sculpture because they idealise our actual experience, whereas it 'arches over this existence with another and diviner (*Letters,* I, 247).

Both hearing and creating music figure prominently not only in *The Spanish Gypsy* but in *The Legend of Jubal and Other Poems.* 'Armgart' tells of a singer who loses her voice, and hence her hope of worldly fame, and finds gratification serving her own servant. In 'Stradivarius' the great violin-maker imparts 'responsive life' to his instruments and is 'living in the air' whenever they are played. In 'How Lisa Loved the King' it is a musician acting as a priestly confessor who convinces the maiden to accept a lesser fate than marriage to the monarch. In 'Arion' the 'melodic soul' who 'taught the dithyramb to roll' sings so passionately just before his death by drowning that his murderers think 'some god was present there'.

Two other poems in the volume bring us closer to the theme of 'The Choir Invisible': the title poem and 'The Death of Moses'. In both, death appears in the guise of a blessing because of the good the dead can do. Jubal, having invented the lyre, and hence song itself, travels far and wide to proclaim the wonder and 'make the heavens one joy-diffusing choir'. Death alone can purge him of the egotism that accompanies his gift: that egotism dies with his 'fleshly self'. Tombless, he shines 'in man's soul, a god / Who found and gave new passion and new joy / That naught but earth's destruction can destroy'. In 'The Death of Moses'[14] an 'all penetrating' but disembodied voice reveals to the prophet the gift of death, which frees man from the flesh. Moses is denied a burial place precisely so that he may live on everywhere as the law he imparted — a sterner variant of the indwelling presence of the invisible choir. The poem's formal dialogue, angelic messengers, and skyey voyages inevitably recall Milton. 'The Choir Invisible', though without these conscious reverberations of grand style, does undeniably portray a Paradise Attained.

Rather than seeking to justify the ways of God to man, George Eliot is seeking to persuade us of her intimations of immortality. Yet she would probably have accepted for her poem the disclaimer with which Wordsworth prefaced his 'Intimations Ode', calling its myth of pre-existence 'far too shadowy a notion to be recommended to faith, as more than an element in our instincts of immortality'. She meant her myth of post-existence to be recommended not to faith, with its dogmatic implications, but to morality. While repudiating the notion that loss of faith in an objective future life robbed man of his moral sense (*Letters*, VI, 97–100), she sought at the same time to strengthen the grounds of morality for those deprived of the old motivation. Religion might do its part, but only if it preached 'less care for personal consolation, and a more deeply-awing sense of responsibility to man', attitudes Pantheism could not inspire because it required viewing the universe 'from the outside of our relations to it . . . as human beings' (*Letters*, v, 31). Yet her conception of the Choir Invisible drew upon the pantheistic understanding of an indwelling presence. Like the 'still, sad music of humanity' which in 'Tintern Abbey' is said to disturb man 'with the joy / Of elevated thoughts', the strains of her choir have 'ample power / To chasten and subdue'. They are, however, found not in 'the round ocean and the living air', but exclusively in 'the mind of man'.

We know that from her youth George Eliot found strength, as so many others did, in Wordsworth's healing power; that she read him in the last months of her life, when grief and new love mingled; and that he provided more epigraphs for her novels than did any other writer besides Shakespeare, herself excepted.[15] Although she freely composed her own epigraphs if the work of others failed to answer her needs, when pressed by Frederic Harrison to suggest inspirational readings for the Positivists in the spring of 1880, she did not recommend her own works but Wordsworth's. Even the Positivists may not have noted that the passages she suggested echoed certain themes of 'The Choir Invisible'. One, from *The Prelude*, speaks of human nature as 'a spirit / Diffused through time and space'; another of the 'one great society alone on Earth: / The noble Living and the noble Dead'. And she told Harrison she knew nothing finer than the closing lines of the sonnet 'Toussaint l'Ouverture', which proclaim the presence of 'powers' that would work for the martyred revolutionary: 'Exultations and agonies / And Love, and man's unconquerable mind (*Letters*, vii, 261 – 2).

One of the last new books George Eliot read was a study of Wordsworth by her friend Frederic W. H. Myers, the poet and student of psychic phenomena (*Letters*, vii, 342). Against his hope of finding empirical evidence of a spirit world we can set hers of imaginatively depicting one that required no research and violated no laws of nature. If his motives were scientific, hers were moral: and the intensity of her concern is evident in her famous Kantian pronouncements to him in the Fellows' garden of Trinity College, Cambridge, on how 'inconceivable' was the notion of God, how 'unbelievable' that of Immortality, and 'yet how peremptory and absolute' that of Duty. To Myers her words seemed to withdraw from his grasp 'the two scrolls of promise, leaving only the third'.[16] But does not 'The Choir Invisible' restore some part of the second promise in language reminiscent of the poet they both loved?

And is it not likely that painting as well as poetry and music helped to inform George Eliot's conception of the Choir Invisible? *The Spanish Gypsy* and *Romola* were both begun partly in consequence of her being moved by a painting; and she even once remarked of the colours in a Burne-Jones canvas: 'They are poems'.[17] 'Paint us an angel, if you can', says the narrator in *Adam Bede*; and 'paint us yet oftener a Madonna', he adds; but then comes the famous repudiation of any aesthetic canon that would 'banish from the region of Art' images of 'old women scraping carrots with work-worn hands' (Ch. 17). 'The Choir Invisible' surely was meant to include and exalt not only spiritual heroes but all such uncomely anonymous toilers, whose 'unhistoric acts' (to use the closing words of *Middlemarch*) add to 'the growing good of the world'. But of course the poem more obviously evokes glorious images from the art of the Middle Ages, the Renaissance, and the Baroque — angels, cherubs, saints, madonnas. There are indeed suggestive parallels between its transcendent yet indwelling host of sanctified spirits and the subjects of certain paintings in which George Eliot took a great interest during her European travels. In Titian's 'Assumption of the Virgin', in Venice, Raphael's 'Coronation of the Virgin', in Rome, Overbeck's 'Triumph of Christianity in the Arts', in Frankfurt, and many other works she doubtless knew, a radiant cloudborne host, some celestial or eternal order, co-exists with the temporal order, embodying its aspirations and inspiring its life.[18]

Heavenly hosts in European paintings may have provided inspiration for 'The Choir Invisible', but the madonna figure so often seen in such pictorial groups is absent from George Eliot's conception. Her choir lacks individuation, hierarchy — and, one might say, a soloist. We know how highly she and Lewes valued Raphael's Sistine Madonna, which they studied daily for weeks in Dresden in 1858 and considered a consummate image of ideal humanity (*Letters*, ii, 471–2; Haight, p. 264). And we recall that in *The Mill on the Floss* Philip tells Maggie that Raphael's 'mysteriously divine child' in the arms of the Madonna affects the beholder as mysteriously as music (Bk. vi, Ch. 1). We must also assume that George Eliot was well aware of the role assigned to the madonna in Auguste Comte's Religion of Humanity. Benign and majestic, as befits a goddess, a spouseless mother in flowing robes cradles an infant of indeterminate sex: so symbolised on banners and emblems, Humanity nurturing its own future would be the ultimate object of public worship in the Positivist era.[19]

George Eliot's failure to use the image of the madonna, the central icon of the Religion of Humanity, may suggest a certain larger ambivalence toward the Positivist teaching that 'The Choir Invisible' has always been said to embody. Though she is increasingly seen by scholars to have been deeply influenced by Positivism, no-one has critically assessed the doctrinal content of her most 'positivist' poem. To do so is to find that it comes closest to Comte's conception of a new religion in its reliance on memory and meditation as agents of grace and its idealisation of the dead as inspiration for the living—termed by Comte 'subjective immortality'. His concomitant assumptions George Eliot also shares: that only the worthy survive in memory and only the good influences the future. And Comte's maxims, 'Live for others', and 'The living are more and more governed by the dead', are implicit in the poem.

Yet 'The Choir Invisible' is far from being an adequate expression of the Religion of Humanity or a reliable guide to its implications. The poem contains no suggestion of the worship of corporate Humanity as *Le Grand Être*, symbolised by the madonna, nor of the public and private forms of the cultus (private worship, for men only, included prayers to man's three Guardian Angels, mother, wife and daughter, appropriate substitutions being allowable). It makes no reference to a universal, hierarchical, authoritative Positivist church which mediates between the living and the dead and organises all life in rigid patterns of obligation (*Polity*, I, 283–5; II, 55, 106; III, 136, 408–9, 470, 530; IV, 76–140). 'Joining' her Choir seems automatic for all the deserving: there is nothing of Comte's sacrament of Incorporation performed seven years after death by a priest of Humanity to certify participation in the Great Being by men—women and useful animals being included as auxiliaries without benefit of sacrament (*Polity*, IV, 33, 100, 115, 312; *Catechism*, pp. 95–6). Nor does 'The Choir Invisible' teach the extreme rationale for moral conduct that Comte had arrived at when he wrote that man's life was 'nothing but a trial of his worthiness for the final incorporation [in the Great Being]' (*Polity*, II, 54). And finally, unconcerned with human epochs and cultures, with race, creed, age, and sex, George Eliot implies a universalism that Comte's parochial perspective precluded. (His Positivist Calendar [*Policy*, IV, 346–51], a kind of minimal Choir of the noble dead – 558 members – is heavily male, European, and Gallic). Like many others who genuinely found inspiration in Comte, George Eliot evidently perceived embarrassing, puzzling, and indeed ominous tendencies of thought as well. Ignoring them proved philosophically and poetically necessary.

Apart from what she did and did not draw from Comte, there is the further question of what George Eliot added. Her poem expresses, elicits, and depends upon strong emotion. Comte, for all his claims of having arrived at the idea of subjective immortality by the inspiration of his love for the dead Clotilde de Vaux, writes in an emotionally sterile idiom; his obsessive systematising drains the affective lifeblood from one arresting conception after another. George Eliot's great controlling metaphor of the Choir surely arises from her own musical sensibility and imagination, not the philosopher's. Her distinction between a baser and a 'rarer, better, truer self' is one Comte hardly entertained, for he eschewed psychology, never lived to write on ethics, and, in any case, assumed that with the advent of the Positivist era all lapses from ideal morality would vanish. And while Comte could not conceive of the Great Being as anything but eternal, or his system as anything but final, George Eliot, at the close of her second strophe, bravely acknowledges the obvious: that the limits of human ideals are fixed by the exigencies of human existence.

With all this in mind we can understand why George Eliot was careful not to let the Positivists engage her talents fully. She declined to write the Positivist novel that Frederic Harrison outlined for her in 1866 (*Letters*, IV, 284–9, 300–2), or to meet his request for Positivist prayers from her pen eleven years later (*Letters*, IX, 194–5; VI, 387–8), although by then she had produced epigrams and tendentious passages enough to suggest that the task should have been congenial. He tried to strengthen his case on that occasion by informing her that Richard Congreve, her old friend and the Positivists' leader, had already quoted from 'The Choir Invisible' in an address, and that the Broad Churchman Llewellyn Davies saw in it the 'germ of a new Hymnology'. Yet recommending Wordsworth was the closest she would come to putting her talents deliberately at the service of the Positivists (*Letters*, VII, 261–2). Her regular but modest contributions to Congreve's Positivist centre in Chapel Street, and occasional attendance at its meetings, are evidence more of her friendship with the chief London Positivists than of any wish to be considered by them (or by the world) as a true believer.

Nor did they claim her as such. Writing to Pierre Laffitte, head of the Paris Positivists, to inform him of George Eliot's death, Frederic Harrison mentioned her unwillingness to accept their religious system, even while noting that they had only recently used her 'noble verses on subjective immortality' at the funeral of a follower.[20] Another of her Positivist friends, Professor E. S. Beesly, said in his New Year's Day 1881 address to his colleagues a few days later that, though she had rejected details in Comte's system, she had found in it a 'refuge from mere negativism'. He then put the Positivist *imprimatur* on her poem by calling it 'the clearest, and at the same time the most beautiful, expression that has yet been given to one of the most distinctive doctrines of Positivism'. And he predicted that it would 'enter into Positivist liturgies of all countries and through all time.[21]

The expansiveness of Beesly's remarks can be attributed to the sentiment of the occasion, but also to the optimism of the London Positivists. By early 1881 there were groups loosely affiliated with them in England, the Continent, South America, and even India (where 'The Choir Invisible' soon entered the liturgy).[22] And just then Beesly and Harrison were preparing to open a new centre in London to rival Congreve's, from which they had seceded. It would be called Newton Hall, and among its sacred texts would be 'The Choir Invisible'. Mrs Harrison, who was in charge of Newton Hall's music, included the work in a volume of 144 poems used in services there or for private devotions; the book, published in 1890, had a title that appropriately expressed George Eliot's theme: *Service of Man*. The writers were as diverse as Blake and Newman, Dante and Wordsworth, Wesley and Shelley, but at least a dozen selections seem to owe their inspiration to George Eliot's poem, if not directly to Comte. One work, on immortality, by her friend W. M. W. Call, even had as its epigraph her words, 'To make undying music in the world'.[23] Eventually her poem found its way into the Liverpool Positivists' hyperorthodox Comtean liturgy, there sharing honours with paeans to the Great Being and the Blessed Human Trinity, dechristianised Anglican hymns invoking Humanity ('Holy, Holy, Holy! Mother pure and mighty!'), a hymn addressed to Comte, an anthem for the Festival of Holy Women, and a chant — 'Ave Clotilde!'[24]

Though commonly regarded not only as a Positivist poem, but also as a Positivist hymn, 'The Choir Invisible' was in fact probably not much sung by Comtist congregations. Its blank verse and extended thought patterns made it difficult and untraditional, but it would have served as a choir anthem. The only known musical setting composed specifically for the Positivists was a cantata employing a full choir of mixed voices and featuring a baritone solo and quartet accompanied by double string quartets and contrabass. This large and complex work was by Henry Holmes, symphonic composer, concert violinist, and Professor of Violin at the Royal College of Music, who had once been invited by George Eliot to play at the Priory (*Letters*, vi, 370). He conducted its single known performance, at Newton Hall, appropriately on the last day of December, the Day of All the Dead in Comte's Calendar.[25] We know that hearing her own words from *The Spanish Gypsy* sung by John Cross' sister affected George Eliot deeply (Cross, p. 452), and that she was much moved by choral works. How regrettable it is, then, that this performance of the Holmes cantata took place three years after her death — and that the score seems to have disappeared.

Fortunately, at least six other musical settings exist. Two are by women, Josephine Troup[26] and Edith Swepstone,[27] both prolific composers of music for popular Victorian poetry. Each severely truncated the poem, Troup using only the first and third strophes, Swepstone only the first. Yet both compositions are musically demanding enough to suggest that they were probably sung by choirs as anthems rather than by congregation as hymns, though they appear in hymn books published by London ethical societies just after the turn of the century. The poem's earnest, creedless altruism perfectly suited such groups. They had grown out of Unitarianism, which itself had lost much of its Christian character during George Eliot's lifetime, partly due to two Unitarian ministers well known to her: James Martineau, who wrote for the *Westminster Review* when she edited it, and Thomas Sadler, who officiated at her funeral and Lewes's.[28] At least one published Unitarian funeral service contained her poem by 1882,[29] as did a Unitarian service and chant book of 1913.[30]

'The Choir Invisible' has proved equally appropriate for more secular musical purposes. In 1882 Edward Hecht, Bavarian-born assistant director of the Halle Orchestra in Manchester, used the poem's complete text for a cantata requiring perhaps fifty voices, a solo quartet, and full orchestra.[31] Ambitious in another way, John More Smieton in 1889 set the poem's first thirteen lines to music for the Dundee Glee Choir, calling for an organ obbligato and two separate choral groups, one hidden from the audience — truly an invisible choir.[32] When Girton College acquired a new organ for its chapel in 1910, Cyril Bradley Rootham, organist, composer, and musical director of St John's College, Cambridge, perhaps recalled that George Eliot had contributed to the foundation of the women's college forty years before. In any case, for the dedication of the instrument he composed an extended work for women's choir, soprano solo and organ based on the first eleven lines of 'The Choir Invisible'.[33] And finally, John Joubert, composer and Professor of Music at Birmingham University, has written a choral symphony in a modern idiom inspired by humanistic conceptions of immortality. The texts of its first two movements, 'Let us now praise famous men', from Ecclesiastes, and Stephen Spender's 'I Think Continually of Those Who Were Truly Great', culminate in a third movement whose exalted words are George Eliot's.[34]

All these composers have given her vision of subjective immortality new meaning and effect: to her sense they have added their sound. Rendering *The Choir Invisible* audible may once have made its message more credible to the ears of faith. Whether or not we today are persuaded, we may still be moved and elevated by her poem. It deserves to survive its current neglect and to be read once more as a touchstone of humanist piety in the Victorian age.

NOTES

1   But see George William Creel, 'The Poetry of George Eliot', Diss. University of California, Los Angeles, 1948; Cynthia Ann Secor, 'The Poems of George Eliot: A Critical Edition with Introduction and Notes', Diss. Cornell University, 1969; and David H. Siff, 'The Choir Invisible: The Relation of George Eliot's Poetry and Fiction', Diss. New York University, 1968.
2   GE to William Blackwood, 6 March 1874, *The George Eliot Letters*, 9 vols,

ed. G.S. Haight (New Haven: Yale University Press, 1954–78), VI, 26 (hereafter cited as *Letters*).

3 Cicero, *Letters to Atticus*, trans, E. O. Winstedt, in Loeb's Classical Library, 3 vols (Cambridge: Harvard University Press, 1961), III, 35, letter XII, part 18.

4 Spencer to Frederic Harrison, 26 December 1880, Harrison Collection, Library of Political and Economic Science, London School of Economics; Gordon S. Haight, *George Eliot: A Biography* (Oxford: The Clarendon Press, 1968), p. 522 (hereafter cited as Haight); *Letters*, IX, 262 (quoting Edith Simcox's words).

5 Printing Sadler's address, the editor of *Transactions of the Unitarian Historical Society*, 5 (1932), 203–6, called the passage quoting the poem 'difficult to read'; Haight, in *Letters*, IX, 324, citing the *Daily News*, 30 December 1880, notes Sadler's alteration of 'immortal dead who live again' to 'who still live on'. I find no evidence that the poem was sung, much less at the graveside, as asserted by Marghanita Laski, *George Eliot and Her World* (London: Thames and Hudson, 1973), p. 115.

6 Creel, p. 105, makes this point, and Secor, pp. 142–4, notes that the holograph MS in the British Library is dated 1867.

7 Mathilde Blind, *George Eliot*, 2nd edn. (London: W. H. Allen, 1883), p. 169.

8 John D. Jump, *The Ode* (London: Methuen, 1974); George N. Schuster, *The English Ode from Milton to Keats* (1940; rpt. Gloucester, Mass.: Peter Smith, 1964).

9 U.C. Knoepflmacher, *Religious Humanism and the Victorian Novel: George Eliot, Walter Pater, and Samuel Butler* (Princeton: Princeton University Press, 1965), pp. 60–3.

10 On Feuerbach's influence on her see Knoepflmacher, pp. 51–60; Basil Willey, *Nineteenth-Century Studies: Coleridge to Matthew Arnold* (London: Chatto and Windus, 1950), pp. 227–36; Michael Wolff, 'Marian Evans to George Eliot: the Moral and Intellectual Foundations of her Career', Diss. Princeton University, 1958, pp. 207–10, Acton MS 5019, fols 358, 641–2, 645, 735, 984, but on the decline of that influence, fols 767, 822, 1596, Cambridge University Library.

11 William Empson, *Seven Types of Ambiguity* (New York: New Directions, 1949), pp. 152–4.

12 Michael Wolff, 'Tennyson's "Maud"', *Westminster Review*, 64 (October 1855), 596–601, in *Essays of George Eliot*, ed. Thomas Pinney (New York: Columbia University Press, 1963), p. 191; Wolff, pp. 280–1.

13 See Creel, Ch. 3; William J. Sullivan, *George Eliot and the Fine Arts*, Diss. University of Wisconsin, 1970, Ch. 2; Percy M. Young, 'George Eliot and Music', *Music and Letters*, 24 (April 1943), 92–100.

14 The poem appeared first in the Cabinet Edition in 1878 with three other poems not in the 1874 edition.

15 Thomas Pinney, 'George Eliot's Reading of Wordsworth', *Victorian Newsletter*, 24 (1963), 20–2; Secor, p. 70; Creel, pp. 26, 28; David L. Higdon, 'George Eliot and the Art of the Epigraph', *Nineteenth-Century Fiction*, 25 (1970), 127–51.

16 F. W. H. Myers, *Essays Modern*, 2nd edn. (London: Macmillan, 1885), pp. 268–9.

17 John W. Cross, *George Eliot's Life as Related in her Letters and Journals*,

new edn. [1885] (rpt. New York: AMS Press, 1965), pp. 424, 451; *Letters*, III, 295, cited in Sullivan, p. 25.

18 Besides Sullivan, see Hugh Witemeyer, *George Eliot and the Visual Arts* (New Haven and London: Yale University Press, 1979); Haight, pp. 151–2.

19 Auguste Comte, *System of Positive Polity*, 4 vols translated by John Henry Bridges *et al.*, 1875–7 (rpt. New York: Burt Franklin, n.d.), II, 56–7, IV, 96–7, 139, 359, 481. See also Auguste Comte, *The Catechism of Positive Religion*, translated by Richard Congreve (1858, 3rd edn., rev., 1891; rpt. Clifton, New Jersey: Augustus M. Kelley, 1973).

20 Harrison to Laffitte [29 December 1880], Musée d'Auguste Comte, Paris (my translation). For a fuller discussion, see Martha S. Vogeler, 'George Eliot and the Positivists', *Nineteenth-Century Fiction*, Fall 1980.

21 E.S. Beesly, *Some Public Aspects of Positivism: Annual Address....* (London: Reeves and Turner, 1881), p. 7.

22 John Edwin McGee, *A Crusade for Humanity: the History of Organized Positivism in England* (London: Watts & Co., 1931); Geraldine Hancock Forbes, *Positivism in Bengal: A Case Study in the Transmission and Assimilation of an Ideology* (Columbia, Mo.: South Asia Books, 1975), p. 107.

23 W.M.W. Call, *Service of Man: Hymns and Poems*, new edn. (London: Positivist Society, 1908).

24 *Hymns and Anthems for Use in the Church of Humanity* (Liverpool, 1901).

25 For Harrison's address on the occasion, see *The Creed of a Layman: Apologia Pro Fide Mea* (New York: Macmillan, 1907), Ch. 2, misdated 1881 for 1883; the programme is in the Harrison Collection, London School of Economics.

26 Josephine Troup, *Hymns of Modern Thought, Words and Music* (London: South Place Ethical Society, 1912), no. 206. The volume contains two other hymns with lines from her poems, and all three works, without music, are in *Hymns of Modern Thought Used by the Hampstead Ethical Institute* (London: Hampstead Ethical Institute, 1900); *Hymns and Anthems for the Use of South Place Ethical Society, Selected 1889* (London: SPES, n.d.) contains the poem but no music.

27 Edith Swepstone, *Ethical Hymn-Book, with Music*, rev. edn. (London: Council of the Union of Ethical Societies, 1905), no. 105.

28 Horton Davies, *Worship and Theology in England*, IV: *From Newman to Martineau, 1850–1900* (Princeton: Princeton University Press, 1962); S. K. Ratcliffe, *The Story of South Place* (London: Watts & Co., 1955).

29 *A Manual for Use at Funerals* (Boston: George H. Ellis, 1892), with 'C. R. Elliot and C. J. Staples, compilers' written in pencil on the title page and '1886' on its verso, copy at Essex Hall, London, the Unitarian headquarters.

30 *Service and Chant Book* (Halifax: Northgate End Chapel, 1913), copy at Essex Hall and mentioned in Davies, Vol. IV, 270.

31 *O May I Join the Choir Invisible* (London: Novello, Ewer and Co., [1882]).

32 *O May I Join the Choir Invisible* (London: Novello, Ewer and Co.; also New York and Dundee: Methven, Simpson [1889].

33 *Choral Song: O May I Join the Choir Invisible* (London: Stainer and Bell [1910]).

34 *The Choir Invisible ... Opus 54* (London: Novello and Co., 1968). Joubert has also written an opera, *Silas Marner*. For a copy of the symphony and information about the composer, I am indebted to him and his publisher.

8   How George Eliot's People Think

JACOB KORG

As a Positivisit, George Eliot believed that the mind is the product
of a biological evolution analogous to that of the body. She
agreed with G. H. Lewes, who wrote: 'Mind is a successive evolution from experience and its laws are the actions of results. The
Forms of Thought are developed just as the Forms of an Organism are developed'. To George Eliot, the mind and its processes
are emphatically included in the web of cause and effect that constitutes her determined universe. Her marvellously detailed
analyses of thinking reflect this view, for they trace particular
states of mind to antecedent psychological factors.

Yet on the first page of her first story, 'Amos Barton', George
Eliot admits that she does not have a 'well-regulated' mind, and
one suspects that this was an easy confession because she knew
that the mind, though orderly enough from one point of view,
does not lend itself to being well-regulated. And, in fact, our first
encounter with a person's thoughts in her fiction, also in 'Amos
Barton', is a chilling, unsparing confrontation with some of the
least reasonable aspects of the mind. Mrs Patten, a pretty little
old woman of eighty, is serving comfortable tea to comfortable
friends in her comfortable cottage while one of her guests, Mrs
Hackit, is knitting.

> Mrs. Patten does not admire this excessive click-clicking activ-
> ity. Quiescence in an easy-chair, under the sense of compound
> interest perpetually accumulating, has long seemed an ample
> function to her, and she does her malevolence gently.... She
> used to adore her husband and now she adores her money,
> cherishing a quiet blood-relation's hatred for her niece, Janet

Gibbs, who, she knows, expects a large legacy, and whom she is determined to disappoint. Her money shall all go in a lump to a distant relation of her husband's, and Janet shall be saved the trouble of pretending to cry, by finding that she is left with a miserable pittance.[1]

The first qualities of mind we meet in George Eliot's fiction are irritation, avarice and spite.

What is striking about the stream of consciousness, as George Eliot reports it, is its richness and variety. Even Mrs Patten's comparatively simple notions illustrate this. Her thoughts focus on images—Janet stiffly hearing that she has been cut off—but are also compounded of memories, intentions and expectations, and toned by such background feelings as hatred, irritation and satisfaction. As we stroll down the roomy corridors of mental process in George Eliot's more fully realised characters, we are constantly impressed by the mind's ability to move across enormous reaches of space and time, and to assemble the most varied materials into concentrated moments of thought. These become blended with each other into what the modern critic, T. E. Hulme, calls an 'intensive manifold', that is, a complex of things whose parts interpenetrate so thoroughly that they cannot be separated.[2] Hulme uses this term to convey his idea of Bergson's theory of intuitive consciousness, and it is not an accident that it should apply so well to George Eliot's accounts of thinking.

Five hundred years from now readers who compare Joyce's way of rendering mental process in *Ulysses* with George Eliot's descriptions of people thinking will wonder if their characters belonged to the same species. It is hard to believe that both are describing the same function. The interior monologue of Leopold or Molly Bloom is scrappy, paratactic, directionless, without emphasis or a centre of stability, while the thinking of George Eliot's people is reported in complete sentences, often with complex grammatical links, subordination, logical associations and even a balanced structure. Needless to say, the reality both report must be more or less the same, but George Eliot is responding to intellectual imperatives that Joyce has rebelled against. In her prose is reflected the Positivist sense that thought, like everything else, is ordered in an intelligible way. Yet this order, usually perfectly clear to the omniscient intelligence that tells the story, is often invisible to the thinking mind itself, for it is made up of a wide range of impressions, many of them unconscious.

One example of many that might be given occurs in the three pages of psychological analysis dealing with the feelings of Gwendolen Harleth when she comes back from Germany, where she has gone to escape the realisation that she cannot save herself from poverty except by marrying Grandcourt. She arrives alone at the country station, and has to wait in a dirty waiting-room that seems to symbolise her dreary prospects. Outside the door she sees chickens disturbed by the wind. The railway official is strange to her, and has a cast in his eye. The carriage that comes for her is dirty, the man working on it is old. On the ride from the station she reviews her plans for taking her mother abroad, thinks of her four sisters and the dreary household they will make, feels resentment toward Grandcourt for being beyond her reach.[3] It is a compound of immediate sensations, painful memories and dreary expectations, present, past, and future all worked together into a present state of consciousness. It shows the mind as a kind of alchemist's oven which transforms momentary impressions and vague sensations into pronounced states of mind. This alchemy also transforms externals into the counterparts of feelings, a sort of premonition of what is to happen in Symbolist poetry, so that what the preoccupied mind sees in the outer world becomes a vocabulary of its own emotions.

And immediate perception, Bergson tells us, is an abstract of memories. He shows the relation between the mind and actual experience by a diagram of a cone resting its point on a plane.[4] The point is the moment of perception or action or speech when the thoughts, represented by the cone, become overt. The broadening shape of the cone represents the accumulation of thoughts and memories which lies behind any conscious action. The area near the moment of action contains only a few ideas or impulses, but if we were able to pursue the genesis of these, to travel downward to the base of the cone, we would find more and more thoughts involved, until, arriving at the base, we would have to admit that the totality of the contents of the mind is at the root of every action or expression. George Eliot appreciates this perfectly. Speaking of the depressing details Gwendolen sees at the railroad station, she says that trivial things of that kind determine our lives. 'They are continually entering with cumulative force into a mood until it gets the mass and momentum of a theory.'[5]

When Lydgate, in *Middlemarch*, votes for Tyke as the chaplain of the new fever hospital, we are at the point of the cone, the moment of action. Not a word is said about what is going on in Lydgate's mind. But the widening circles of the cone — the thoughts that have controlled his decision — have been made clear earlier. He has spent some time hesitating between Farebrother and Tyke, weighing the merits and defects of each candidate against those of the other, in classical, logical fashion. But his thinking is toned with the feeling that he is above these trivial questions, that he is juggling 'petty alternatives, each of which is repugnant to him'.[6] To understand this, we must go closer to the base of the cone, to the larger circle of Lydgate's general cast of thought, that of an ambitious mind eager to discover the 'primitive tissue', and conscious of high motives, but disfigured by 'spots of commonness' — a feeling of superiority to ordinary matters, and therefore a lack of discrimination about them. We understand that out of all the resources of mind and spirit Lydgate might have brought to his decision, he used the wrong ones, in his haste — his own self-interest and his contempt for what Middlemarch might think of his vote. Later he realises that if he had been objective, he would have voted the other way. Like Bergson, George Eliot understands, and makes us see, that the mind as a whole is involved in every decision.

The plenitude of George Eliot's accounts of thought is best appreciated when it is compared with another method she sometimes uses, one borrowed from Fielding, which treats the mind as the scene of a simple dialectic. In 'Mr. Gilfil's Love Story', Caterina's resentment at the fact that Captain Wybrow is inaccessible to her is expressed through a little dialogue between two imaginary voices. Similarly, the feelings of the oppressed and hate-filled Gwendolen Harleth appear momentarily in the form of a dramatic vignette: 'In Gwendolen's consciousness Temptation and Dread met and stared like two pale phantoms each seeing itself in the other'. But this is quickly followed by a reminder that feelings are never that simple, as George Eliot adds, 'all the while her fuller self beheld the apparitions and sobbed for deliverance from them.[7] That fuller self belongs, of course, to the background personality near the base of Bergson's cone which plays a part in the immediate drama by witnessing it.

George Eliot's gift for grasping the operation of different kinds of minds is displayed in a short and amusing article written for the *Pall Mall Gazette* called 'Servants' Logic', where she analyses the thought processes involved in some of her more exasperating transactions with servants.[8] She notes how difficult it is to get the servant's mind to follow the track of one's own when one is discussing the indigestible fattiness of soup or the problem of imparting a satisfactory polish to the stove. Servants' logic evades the issues, attributes consequences to causes having no relation to them, persists in holding to completely unprovable convictions, takes the laundress for its authority on the weather and current events, and refuses to believe that the same cure for toothache will work for both servants and their employers. George Eliot recognises that it is hopeless to try to change what is, in effect, a separate culture with its own way of thinking.

The empathic power exhibited in 'Servants' Logic' is put to serious use in the novels. For example, when the troubled Hetty Sorrel is meditating flight in *Adam Bede*, her thoughts progress through specific images in a mental idiom appropriate to a frightened and uneducated peasant girl. She thinks of her own possible fate by recalling a young woman with a baby found nearly dead who was taken in by the parish, an image that combines physical suffering with the shame of taking charity. She needs physical objects as cues for thought. Hence, she lays out the jewelery she has brought with her as a reminder of happier times and a source of hope that she may escape destitution for a while. Her decision to go to Dinah for help arises, not from inspiration or calculation, but from the accidental appearance of Dinah's name on the page of a memorandum-book she opens. In a performance that reminds us — at a considerable distance — of the Benjy section of *The Sound and the Fury*, George Eliot subjects herself to a discipline of severe limitation in order to convey the nature of the mind she is for the moment inhabiting.

The minds of George Eliot's people are orderly when considered in the abstract, but not 'well-regulated' because the laws of their operation that are visible to the narrator are concealed from the thinkers themselves. As Karl Kroeber has observed, George Eliot, unlike Charlotte Brontë, employs omniscience to illuminate those parts of a character's mind and motives that we would call unconscious.[9] She was fully aware of this region of the mind. When Gwendolen Harleth, examining her jewelery with the intention of selling it, sets aside the turquoise necklace Daniel Deronda restored to her after she lost it gambling, George Eliot can only say that it was 'something vague and yet mastering which impelled her to this action. . . . There is a great deal of unmapped country within us which would have to be taken into account in an explanation of our gusts and storms.[10] Similarly, when Grandcourt begins to hatch plans about Lush, the companion whom Gwendolen dislikes, George Eliot says: 'We mortals have a strange spiritual chemistry going on within us, so that a lazy stagnation or even a cottony milkiness may be preparing one knows not what biting or explosive material'. A labourer may lack the training 'which makes a character fairly calculable in his actions; but by a roundabout course even a gentleman may make of himself a chancy personage, raising an uncertainty as to what he may do next' — [11] an exceptional situation, clearly.

What we witness, in nearly every important psychological sequence in George Eliot's novels, is the way in which motivations unsuspected by the character, but presented by the narrative intelligence as clear and determinant, even if remote, arise at crucial points to ruin or to rescue the character, in opposition to his original purpose. After her meeting with his former mistress, Gwendolen decides not to marry Grandcourt. The reasons are plain and varied: pride, jealousy, a refusal to do wrong, shame, indignation at being kept out of Grandcourt's secret, offence at being offered a second passion. Yet when he comes to renew his offer, she is surprised to find that she does not want him to leave, and feels an irresistible longing for the financial relief the marriage would bring her and her mother. Grandcourt's remark that he will care for her mother awakens motivations whose power she did not suspect; George Eliot describes her feeling as if all of the settled attitudes were moved from their places and set afloat. Of course, she agrees to marry, and is happy that she will not have to go as a governess.

But then Gwendolen is partially redeemed, not by her conscious will, but by subconscious feelings remote in origin. As she lies wakefully in her bed, she is tormented by an awareness that she has been neutralised as a moral being, that she has shed the structure of her personality as if it were a costume. Now everything she does will seem inconsequential. 'That lawlessness, that casting away of all care for justification, suddenly frightened her . . . all the infiltrated influences of disregarded religious teaching, as well as the deeper impressions of something awful and inexorable enveloping her, seemed to concentrate themselves in the vague conception of avenging powers'.[12] Moral instincts that were 'disregarded' and 'vague' advance into consciousness as a fear that overshadows her expectations of wealth and comfort.

In his 'Preface' to *The Princess Casamassima*, Henry James observes that it is George Eliot's attempt to show the histories of her characters 'as determined by their feelings and the nature of their minds' that makes 'their emotions, their stirred intelligence, their moral consciousness . . . our very own adventure'.[13] After all, it is the character's own awareness of his problem that arouses a corresponding vibration in the reader. But James points out the difficulty this presents to the novelist. The character must know his situation, but must not master it completely, for 'the whole thing comes to depend . . . on the *quality* of bewilderment'.[14] And though James says this with his own Hyacinth Robinson in mind, George Eliot's characters appeal to us in exactly that way. People like Lydgate and Gwendolen strike observers as mature and self-controlled, but at crucial moments parts of their minds that respond to the laws of psychology rather than to their wills come forward. They undergo what James might have called richly tremulous hesitations, are stricken by the truths of their own natures, and drop the reins of their fate. When people with well-regulated minds lose control, they exhibit an exceptionally rare, elevated and pathetic 'quality of bewilderment'. And this becomes one of the sources of that sympathy toward our fellow men that George Eliot so successfully inspires.

NOTES

1   *Scenes of Clerical Life* (Harmondsworth, Penguin Books, 1973), p. 46.
2   T. E. Hulme, 'The Philosophy of Intensive Manifolds', *Speculations*, ed. Herbert Read (New York. n.d. [first published 1924]).
3   *Daniel Deronda*, ed. Barbara Hardy, (Harmondsworth: Penguin Books, 1967), Ch. 21, pp. 268–9.
4   Henri Bergson, *Matter and Memory* (Garden City, 1959), pp. 140–47.
5   *Daniel Deronda*, Ch. 21, p. 269.
6   *Middlemarch*, ed. Gordon S. Haight, (Boston: Houghton Mifflin 1956), Ch. 18, pp. 131–9.
7   *Daniel Deronda*, Ch. 54, p. 738.
8   Reprinted in *Essays of George Eliot*, ed. Thomas Pinney (London: Routledge, 1963), pp. 391–6.
9   Karl Kroeber, *Styles in Fictional Structure* (Princeton, 1971), p. 153–4.
10 *Daniel Deronda*, Ch. 24, p. 321.
11 Ibid., Ch. 28, p. 364.
12 Ibid., Ch. 28, p. 356.

13   Henry James, *The Princess Casamassima* (Harmondsworth, Penguin Books, 1977), p. 16.
14   Ibid., p. 13.

9 George Eliot and the Russians

MIRIAM H. BERLIN

The questions raised by this topic address the unity of European culture in the nineteenth century, the ways literature moved across language barriers, and the specific experience of George Eliot's writings in Russia. The facts offer no radical insights into the artist's intentions, or accomplishment, no brilliant analysis of metaphor or symbol, nor an exegesis on woman's lot in the nineteenth century. This is, instead, an exploration in resonances, a kind of knowledge which might have intrigued our subject herself.

Given the vagaries of cultural migration and the mysterious forces that govern transfer of influences and taste, what kind of reception did George Eliot have among the Russians, and, more important, how did they read her?

The superficial record is immediately arresting: within six months to a year of the publication of her novels in England, they appeared in Moscow or St Petersburg either in serial or book form, often in both, in Russian.[1] This is not surprising, for Russia has been known as English literature's second native land. Shakespeare, Byron, Shelley, Scott, Dickens, Thackeray, the Brontës had evoked extraordinary enthusiasm in the Russian reading public, particularly Dickens and Thackeray, with whom Eliot is always linked, making a warm reception likely for the new literary star of the 1850s. Anglophilism had spread by the end of the eighteenth century through France and Germany to Russia, and in 1772 a satirical journal stated that 'everything English is fine and charming and attracts all of us'.[2] In 1825, Karamzin, poet, historian and novelist, described the family's reading of Walter Scott at night around the tea table (Simmons, pp. 247–8).

The contrast with George Eliot's reception in France is striking. The Russians were enthusiastic, the French virtually indifferent. *Adam Bede* and *The Mill on the Floss* were translated into French within two years of the English publication, but *Romola* took sixteen years, *Middlemarch* nineteen, *Daniel Deronda* five, and *Felix Holt*, though summarised in a journal in the 1860s, has never been issued in book form.[3] The French never wrote about George Eliot with unadulterated appreciation and even the great Taine reflected the general dissatisfaction with his description, 'une grande génie mais artiste incomplète' (Couch, p. 6).

The Russian climate was receptive. Why? What were the elements of Eliot's art that attracted so much attention? This is only half the question, for the answer lies as much with Russian needs and the role of literature in Russia. In 1847, Belinsky, the literary critic, in his famous open 'Letter to Gogol', declared that 'only in literature, in spite of our Tartar censorship, is there still some life and forward movement. . . . This is why the writer's calling enjoys such respect among us'. Here, he spoke of the particular responsibility of Russian writers towards the special burdens that literature had to bear: its function as the only conduit for social and political comment, its uses as a forum for otherwise forbidden discourse. Literature alone in mid-century Russia bore witness to the truth. The emancipation decade of the 1860s transformed the face of society and propelled the question of the people, the *narod*, to centre-stage. Everyone and everything took sides. George Eliot's works, for instance, were published not in the leading radical journals of the sixties, but in one whose interests were aesthetic and politics moderate, and in another known as the conservative journal of Anglophilia (Andreeva, 47–8). But the first critical article on Eliot appeared in a radical journal, *Sovremennik*, and was written by a revolutionary poet.

Since all this bespeaks a heavily political and aesthetically utilitarian environment for literature, what accounted for the attraction of the so-called 'bookish' author who, in every novel, perceived the cause of 'conflict to be moral imperfection'? (Andreeva, 49).

Beyond the Anglomania and general love of English literature the Russians admired the artistry of her language, even in trans-lation: the particularity of detail, the specific gravity of descriptive power, and the subjects themselves — people of the countryside, people of the land. What was called her 'domestic realism' contrasted with the harsher satire of her English predecessors and the crude 'naturalism' of the French school. The radicals found common cause with her concrete, affectionate, respecting and revealing, detailed, specific concern with the people; the aestheticians delighted in the deft, sharp, precise skill in using language to bring imagination to life, and the conservatives thrilled to so faithful a depiction of the English landscape, both natural and social.

Swept along, then, to some degree by what had come before her, responsive to the varied needs of the period, George Eliot was particularly popular in Russia in the 1860s and 1870s.

Mikhailov, revolutionary poet, translator of Heine, Béranger, and Hugo, who gave his life in Siberia, when revising *Adam Bede* in October 1859 raised certain questions characteristic of Eliot criticism in Russia for the ensuing century. First, there was the word, the problem of translation. Without evaluating the Russian renditions, suffice it to say that what the Russians received was not always what had been intended. Dickens had in Vvedinskii a translator who booked himself as co-author. He felt so at one with the spirit of Dickens that he often substituted Russian characteristics, modes of address, even phraseology that may have altered the letter but kept the freshness and humour of the original in ways which more accurate twentieth-century translations have failed to do.[5] Between such changed passages and the intervention of the censor where the slightest hint of 'sedition' was present, whole pages might be altered. Eliot, with no such self-appointed or commonly recognised Russian counterpart, was subject to artistic indignities along with all the other authors.[6]

Then there was the problem of critics who judged without having read the original. Overriding, perhaps, was the political use of literature and literary criticism in Russia. Developed in the nineteenth century by an increasingly socially conscious and critical intelligentsia battling a deadening and smothering censorship and bureaucracy, the legacy of the political use of literature is well known, particularly in the Soviet period. Whatever end the politicisation seeks, it must influence the very perception of literature. And the continuities are manifest.

How does George Eliot fit into this scheme of things? Critical comment has been sporadic. There is not even a baker's dozen of articles, the pattern following that in the West with a certain slackening off at the turn of the century. Eliot scholarship has not been a first priority for the Russians, but there are some fascinating perceptions illuminating Russian interests more, perhaps, than the Victorian. I should like to look at these areas: specific literary comment, assessment by Russia's great literary giants, and memoir material.

Mikhailov's review of *Adam Bede*[7] published in 1859 echoes *The Times* and *Westminster Review* in stating that Eliot's greatness lies in her ability to 'give life to the experience of the most insignificant as well as the heroes of her drama',[8] and noting that the external action is much less interesting than the internal life of the characters. Summarising the story, he translates in full the scenes in which Dinah tells Mr Irwine how she came to preach and the passage describing Hetty's beauty, particularly remarking the almost physiological detail along with the poetic expression. He points out that he could make a whole book of quotations to show the marvels of the author's language (Mikhailov, p. 120). The climax of this paean is the prison scene between Dinah and Hetty (Mikhailov, p. 126).

Eliot's language raises conflicting questions for Mikhailov. On the one hand she is the rival of the best masters of the Flemish school . . . the marvellous simplicity of detail and everything act on the reader more strongly than a coup de théâtre or bright colours (Mikhailov, p. 128). At the same time, though admiring the specificity, he asks if the foreign reader not fully acquainted with English dialect might not object to the extensive use of localisms, or whether this does not actually deprive the work of true art. 'Would it not produce an unhappy impression on a Russian reader if the story set in Belorussia had all the people speaking in pidgin Belorussian dialect? 'Didna' instead of did not, 'gell' instead of girl . . . ought not to be there. It is one thing to collect some particularly marked idioms, but to take note of each one's way of pronouncing—this leads to nothing' (Mikhailov, p. 110). He mentions Donnithorne's sudden appearance, a *deus ex machina*, as a defect, a kind of banality—though, admittedly, the only one in three volumes.

Mikhailov's review set the tone for the Russian commentators: admiring, generous, and quite specific. Always noting the marvels of the language, the critics emphasise Eliot's particular kind of realism which the specificity of language renders so brilliantly. This so-called 'domestic realism', greater if not so humorous as

Dickens's, was not so negative as Thackeray's, and created a novel 'of character', as Tsebrikova wrote in 1871,

> possible only in the country of Anglo-Saxon individualism. Only there, where personality is so highly developed, where law gives full play to all powers, where the study of free will is so rooted, could a novel emerge whose intention is the deep and detailed analysis of all the moral powers from which the personality is formed.[9]

But it was that uncanny capacity to observe and render detail like the Flemish masters in combination with a particular philosophical posture whose success the Russians have judged variously. Tsebrikova said that Eliot lacked tendentiousness, there were no moral admonitions on every page, the reader empathises and sympathises with her characters. Here is not only the 'narrow, constricting realism of the Flemish school; she penetrates into the human soul . . . shows us people — her realism consists in escaping falsity and romanticism, and holds strictly to the truth of life' (Tsebrikova, 176).

In 1891 Davydova argues that Eliot's intent was to awaken the reader's sympathy towards the people, and to do this she dwelt on the life of the lower classes, 'doing for the peasantry what Dickens did for the bourgeoisie and Thackeray for the aristocracy'.[10] The philosophy that this precision of observation and artistry serves Davydova calls 'meliorism': 'Eliot believed that future progress would be in the accumulation of knowledge leading to moral perfection and in the course of time the great sum of human suffering would be diminished' (Davydova, 80).

Boborykin, the distinguished journalist and writer, who visited Eliot and Lewes in 1868, described Eliot as not young and 'looking very much like that type of Englishwoman who comes to Russia as a governess'. Their salon he found 'most wonderful in its love for intellectual freedom, absence of British "cant" and national or class prejudice'.[11] Writing in 1900 on the European novel in the nineteenth century, he said that the 'unity of scientific spirit with the artistic is the particular mark of George Eliot, and, despite her moral and philosophical inclinations, she was less hindered in the achievement of full artistic harmony than the more objective Dickens and Thackeray'.[12] He noted her Comtian positivist beliefs and counted her among those 'believing in the religion of humanity, for whom the moral basis must be not God's law but the laws of earthly human reality'. But, despite the absence of 'British narrowness or the wish to unmask or mock with a moral goal, and, despite her immense talents of sharp observation and capacity to depict various spheres of life, she did not reach the highest limits of artistic creation'. Why? In the novels 'we do not see the full correspondence between the realism of details and life situations and the creation of particular characters' ('Evropeiskii Roman', pp. 532–3). Her cherished principles and feelings get in the way. Adam Bede, a country carpenter, seems too much a self-taught philosopher. Lydgate, Felix Holt, Silas Marner, with their 'spiritual qualities, staunchness, heroism, uncommon moral purity, are possible as representatives of a highly developed moral person . . . they do not correspond to the background of the picture, the actuality which is the context of the given work'. The women are too idealised. (This is a weakness of the sex.) And the

> swindling, evil, and banal population of Middlemarch is drawn with rich and detailed analysis, revealing in the author a moralist and not an artist, when the highest goal must be the work of art, not the moral. The unity of scientific and artistic development will be achieved when scientific thought uses reality as its base, not intruding into the writing ('Evropeiskii Roman' p. 534).

Kuz'min, a Soviet critic writing in 1956, also feels that positivist ideas prevented Eliot from penetrating into the bases of social conflict. Action is replaced by historical or psychological analysis, diminishing the drama or fabulist quality, making the books boring. The postivist ethic demands 'prosaic life' and the result is works poor in events. If the earlier novels for the century could be called the 'Life and Adventures of', now they might be called 'Life without Adventure'. Eliot presses on the reader a boring and puritanical morality: the example given is Godfrey Cass's childless marriage, which has no other reason than to punish him for the earlier abandonment of his illegitimate child.[13]

Perhaps the most idiosyncratic observation of the Russian and, of course, Soviet critics has to do with the absence of a political-social dimension. But they are not alone, for Quentin Anderson, to mention one, in his Introduction to the *Pelican Guide to English Literature* says that Eliot 'is, in fact, incapable

of suggesting the tone of a given period or historical moment. In
Middlemarch, as in George Eliot generally, change is something
intrusive, an irruption from without'.[14] The issue here is very complex. First, there is her brilliant capacity to render what Anderson
calls the 'primitive tissue of a community'; then the aesthetic of
'domestic realism or moderate realism', the objective positive
description which makes her seem flat in comparison with
Dickens, Thackeray, Brontë, and Gaskell. But this very realism
and concentration on typical people rather than the heroes of the
scorned romantics is the essence of her 'protest' against a society
rooted in inequality; against a reality which diminishes and
humbles people, making them petty and dull. It is not without
reason, argues Kuz'min, that the tragedy of her best female creation, Maggie Tulliver, lies in the fact that she is not like eight out
of one hundred girls in her circle (Kuz'min, p. 398).

Then there is her 'social compromise'. Kuz'min illustrates this
in dividing the works between the earlier and the later novels.
Dating from *Romola* those which took longer to write have a
broader sweep of history, locus, politics and people. But they lack
the freshness and beauty of the earlier works whose narrower
canvas showing the life of the small community contains evidence
of clear class antagonism: the conflicts between the evil representatives of the gentry class; Donnithorne against Adam; the
Cass brothers against Silas Marner; the Squire against the Poysers. In these works,

> despite the brilliant depiction of the simple people as honest,
> sincere, great spirited, with a pure inner world and noble feel-
> ings in contrast to the evil and immoral landowners, Eliot pro-
> pounds the idea that a man must be satisfied with his lot. The
> case of Adam Bede bears out this position; by the end of the
> book, the simple carpenter has become the director of a pro-
> perty. Here is the unequivocal moral view of Eliot: do not try to
> transform society, in the limits of a typical working life the per-
> spectives open to a simple fellow are wide enough (Kuz'min,
> pp. 404–5).

This social compromise is intimately connected with her concern for moral rather than political issues. In *The Mill on the
Floss*, which Turgenev considered her finest work, the Soviet critics, Kuz'min and Andreeva, point to new levels of social aware-

ness: the evil, hitherto negative, principle from outside, dwells not in the gentry figure, but in the bourgeois Wakem, a new type whose egotism, vanity, greed, and hard-heartedness are defined not only by his own nature but as having important social ramifications (Kuz'min, p. 406). Tulliver represents the old patriarchal order; Wakem is a man for a new time (Andreeva, p. 62). Maggie's independence of spirit and intellectual vigour forced her to tear herself from his milieu, but Eliot was not prepared to deal with her passionate nature and compromised with society. Mikhailov had already observed this in 1860:

> *The Mill on the Floss* would be a bitter protest against social and family prejudice, entangling and preparing ruin for even the best and most energetic natures if the author herself did not favor these ideas, or at least try to find something reasonable in them. Miss Evans describes Maggie's suffering and ruin not as the result of despotic stupidity surrounding her; she evidently does not consider Maggie's wishes and aspirations justified . . . she gave her novel such a compromising character out of fear of offending some of the cherished ideas of the society she lives in.[15]

Georg Lukács has said that 'for the inner life of man its essential traits and conflicts can be truly portrayed only in organic connection with social and historical factors'.[16] Here George Eliot has been found wanting. No doubt, Davydova observed in 1891,

> she, herself, always stood on the edge of social and political life, and despite her sympathy, never took part in the socialist activity starting in England in the sixties. She had a completely different nature and was always more interested in questions of art and philosophy than in political and social affairs (Davydova, p. 21).

In *Adam Bede* and 'Mr. Gilfil's Love Story', says Kuz'min, Eliot was so intent on the 'depiction of daily ritual and the psychological collisions of personal life that the reader is unaware of the tumultuous events such as the Irish Rebellion or counter-revolution in France'. Even in *Romola* she has not succeeded in her expressed intention of defining the fate of Tito and Romola by the political and social events of the era, but 'transforms the moral problems of Victorian England and lets escape the chief thing which propelled Savanarola to give social significance to his sermon—the enmity of the people to the power of the Medici' (Kuz'min, p. 410).

In her most political novel, *Felix Holt, the Radical*, Holt, as Henry James has put it, is 'distinguished for his excellent good sense, . . . uncompromising yet moderate, eager yet patient, earnest yet impassioned. He is, indeed, a thorough young Englishman'.[17] But *Felix Holt* is put to interesting use by a radical Russian Jacobin of the 1860s. Tkachev in 1868 wrote an article entitled 'People of the Future and the Heroes of Philistinism'.[18] Holt, needless to say, is one of the people of the future

> whose distinguishing characteristic is that all their activity, even the whole shape of their lives is determined by one wish, by one passionate idea—to make the majority of people happy, to bring as many as possible to the banquet of life. The realization of this idea becomes their sole task, because this idea is completely intertwined with their conception of their own personal happiness (Tkachev, p. 174).

Tkachev used Holt's commitment, his wish to 'share the life of the people and as far as it is in my power to make life less harsh for the poor' to construct the idea of the professional revolutionary, the man whose goal would take precedence over every other aspect of his life. This is what the 'people of the future' would become, and the line to Lenin's *What Is To Be Done* and the Bolshevik cadres is direct. Tkachev argues, 'Seeing in the enlightenment and moral development of the people his sole means of saving them, Holt decides to dedicate his whole life to the task and in order to fulfil it more successfully, he willingly consecrates himself to poverty . . . and chastity' (Tkachev, p. 174).

Holt evoked other responses: in 1871 Tsebrikova wrote that he had more honour in Russia than in England, that George Eliot was the first to reveal the filthy pool of intrigue, venality, drunkenness and incitement of the people through which the aristocracy achieved places in Parliament, and that Holt is a new type whose device, 'service to the people' could only be created by the spirit of English individualism (Tsebrikova, p. 194). Davydova noted that Holt in his sharp manners, rough-hewn ways, and scornful attitude towards contemporary mores, is reminiscent of the nihilists, like Sazarov in Turgenev's *Father and Sons* (Davydova, p. 60). Karl Marx had some pointed words about Felix Holt, the *Rascal*. On 10 June 1869 he wrote to his daughter, Jenny, about a survey engineer named Dykens:

> Something on the order of Felix Holt without the affectation, but with the knowledge. He invites the factory fellows once a week, treats them to beer and tobacco, and talks with them about social themes. He is a communist 'by instinct'. I certainly would not refrain from joking with him about meeting Missis [sic] Eliot who would immediately seize him and transform him into her literary substance (Kuz'min, p. 412).

Middlemarch and *Daniel Deronda* did not receive as much particular attention. Eliot's commitment to the moral transformation of society is again seen as the force that propels Ladislaw, Dorothea, and Deronda to serve society as they do. Eliot's proclivities for moral teaching and political scepticism require her to place their hopes on the moral transformation of society and humanity (Boborykin, *Vospominaniia*, ii, 411). Maxim Gorkii had a word about her commitment to the 'little village as a social organism':

> George Eliot's boring book, *Middlemarch*, and the books of Auerbach and Spielhagen showed me that in the English and German provinces people live not exactly as on Zvezdinskii Street in Nizhni-Novgorod, but not much better. They talk about their English and German kopeks, about the fear and love of God; but, just as the people of my street, they do not love one another, and, most particularly, dislike those who are different in any way (Kuz'min, p. 414).

Several critics noted in *Middlemarch* a streak of satire absent in her other works, along with a sharpened use of the idea of the power of money over man. In *Daniel Deronda*, Kuz'min points to impressionist psychology and symbolism as a new device. The two plot lines of the book are briefly discussed, Deronda's great work is described as the fight against anti-semitism, but nowhere is it stated that he is a Jew or that his vision was for a Jewish homeland. Kuz'min's essay appeared in 1955, just after Stalin's death and the anti-semitic Doctor's Plot in Moscow.

The Soviet critics especially remark Eliot's use of the discoveries of Spencer, Darwin, and Huxley. She 'subscribed to the principle that determinism formed the fate of people and strove to draw society as an organism developing from natural evolution'.[19] Given the taboos of Victorian culture, her interest in biology and physiology had to be masked in her work, but it was present in her heroes: in Adam Bede, the working of the 'inalienable nature of his being'; in *Middlemarch*, the cameo portrait revealing Ladislaw as the son of his mother in looks, personality and fate (Ivasheva, p. 111). The relationship of human actions to the surrounding circumstances is considered a kind of dialectic, the result of a biological conflict between the strong and the weak, as in the case of Wakem and farmer Tulliver; and the result of biological determinism, as in the case of Maggie, farmer Tulliver's daughter, and Tom, mother Dodson's son (Ivasheva, p. 115). Eliot, unlike Dickens, had no wish to deal with the outside world. The ethical questions she raises and the positivist impulse towards the virtual physicalisation of things as they are mark her originality. Ivasheva and Andreeva argue from this that Zola's programme of naturalism, formulated with the decade, was not the first; Eliot was the representative of the English variant of naturalism (Ivasheva, p. 110; Andreeva, p. 45).

Are there any insights or reflections on women in the Russian treatment of George Eliot? The question has a certain poignancy, for the 'woman question' in underdeveloped Russia was a vital part of the larger emancipation era of the 1860s. Different uses are made of Eliot's being a woman. Boborykin notes that the new element of intellectual synthesis in English literature has come from a woman. Tsebrikova says in 1871 that women writers are not up to Thackeray's merciless satire and are distinguished by

idealisation and preference for one side of life, the English clergy. The pastors are shown, in the ideal personalities of the apostles . . . . this spirit of clericalism is so deeply imbedded in the female mind, not as a consequence of its peculiar qualities, but of the conditions of feminine life . . . even George Eliot . . . despite her own realism has paid her fee to this spirit, and only in her last novel, *Felix Holt*, gave a type of heroine who found an idea of life apart from clericalism. Esther becomes the wife-helper of a man who is not distinguished by a particular respect towards bishops and archbishops (Tsebrikova, p. 201).

And herein lies the catch: a wife-helper. Despite the contrast in human types, in freedom of moral choice, between Mrs Transome and Esther, in the name of what, asks Tkachev, has Esther sacrificed her luxurious life? She gives herself to ideas because her beloved holds them (Tkschev, pp. 226–7). 'I do not wish you to study,' says Mr Tulliver to Maggie. 'If a woman wants to be actually free,' says Felix Holt, 'let her show her strength to choose something better; if not, let her be led by the ideas of her father or husband.' Eliot's own life flouted these strictures, made what Tsebrikova calls that 'transition from weak creature to thinking being', though, unlike George Sand, she did not use this rich source of ideas and images towards propaganda for the liberation of women. But, 'the English mind permits propaganda only for missionary societies and the free distribution of different edifying books' (Tsebrikova, p. 202). What effect being a woman had on her art is a different issue. For the most part critics note that Eliot is the exception among women writers in knowing how to create men, despite which, her women are better.

On a quite different level is the personal memoir of Sophia Kovalevskaia, Professor of Mathematics in Stockholm. Welcomed at the Priory as a young student from Berlin on a Sunday afternoon in 1869, she was presented by George Eliot to an elderly gentleman with 'a typical English face and grey whiskers'. Eliot said to this unnamed gentleman, 'I am so glad that you have come today, for here is the living refutation of your theory that women are incapable of abstract thought; here is a woman mathematician'. A spirited conversation followed, the young Russian heatedly discoursing on issues of woman's emancipation, education and freedom to choose, all arguments she had so recently used to obtain her own family's permission to study in Berlin. After three-quarters of an hour, during which all other conversation had ceased, George Eliot commended her on the intelligence and courage of her debate and said 'If Herbert Spencer is not now convinced, we shall have to judge him prejudiced'.[20]

Turning from the woman question to the particular woman, what was the assessment of Eliot's work by Russia's great literary figures? We know that Turgenev was a warm acquaintance. There are scattered references in her letters and his to their meetings, and a touching note of condolence to her on George Lewes's death: 'May you find in your own great mind the necessary fortitude to sustain such a loss. All your friends, all learned Europe mourn with you', he wrote from Paris, 3 December 1878.[21] A greater admirer and judge of female beauty, Turgenev said that Eliot was the woman who made it possible for him to see that he could fall madly in love with someone who was admittedly not beautiful (Kovalevskaia, p. 96).

Tolstoi never met George Eliot, but his regard for her genius is well known. In *What is Art* he places *Adam Bede* in the category of the most important art of our time.[22] On 11 October 1859, he wrote in a letter 'I read *Adam Bede*. Powerfully tragic, although wrong and full of one idea'.[23] In June of that year he had written to his brother,

> If you were in Russia now I would send you Eliot's *Scenes from Clerical Life*. Now, I beg you to scan it, particularly 'Janet's Repentance'. People like the English are blessed, who with their milk suck up Christian learning and in the high and rarefied form of evangelical protestantism. This is a moral and religious book (Tolstoi, pp. 60, 300).

In a letter to his wife in 1885 he wrote:

> I am reading Eliot's *Felix Holt*. Marvelous contents. This is a thing that ought to be translated if it is not yet. That would be a joy. I have not yet finished and I am afraid the ending will be spoiled. My brother Serezha gave it to me. Tell him everything he said about the book is true (Tolstoi, 83, 477).

Tolstoi places Eliot's works on his list of books that had made a 'great impression' on him. The library at Yasnaya Polyana has on its shelves *Adam Bede, Felix Holt, Romola, The Mill on the Floss* and *Middlemarch*. The first three contain notes in Tolstoi's hand.

Among his 'aphorisms for the soul' Tolstoi quotes four times Eliot's comment,

> There is no harsh deed for which the doer alone is punished. We cannot act without sharing our evil deeds with others. Our deeds, good and bad, are like our children: they live and act not just by our will, but on their own (Tolstoi, 40, p. 366; 41, p. 491; 43, p. 309; 45, p. 58).

In his article on *Adam Bede* and *Anna Karenina* W.C. Gareth
Jones takes great pains to show certain parallels between Hetty
and Anna, Donnithorne and Vronsky, the harvest scene in
Poyser's Great Meadow and Levin's Bol'shoi Lug (Great
Meadow), Hetty's contemplated and Anna's actual sucide. No
greater compliment could be paid than such a stimulus for
artistic invention. This is not to say that Tolstoi states the proven-
ance of these elements, but the inferential argument is persua-
sive.[24]

One personal memoir is of great interest. Sophia Kovalevskaia
reported on a later visit to George Eliot and John Cross two weeks
before Eliot's death. Professor Haight says that this visit, not listed
in Eliot's diary, did not take place,[25] but in her memoir
Kovalevskaia speaks with great specificity about her hesitation in
visiting the great writer in this new and seemingly anomalous
marriage. The Russian visitor found George Eliot and John Cross
so affectionate and companionable together that she quite lost
her prejudice; she found their chambers so much more delightful
and charming than the larger and gloomier rooms of the Priory
that the whole effect was idyllic. In this last conversation she
voiced a long-held perplexity: how is it that in all the novels the
complex, difficult problems of human relations are resolved by
death? She had always wondered how Maggie would have dealt
with her powerful passions if she had not drowned? Would she
have internalised them, used them to help others? What would
have become of her? and Dorothea if Causaubon had lived for
twenty years more? or Gwendolen if she had had to endure a lifetime with Grandcourt? George Eliot replied: 'Have you not found
that life, itself, often provides unexpected possibilities and resolutions through death? Indeed, for me it has often been the
certitude of death that has given me the courage to live' (Kovalevskaia, p. 108).

What has this exercise in sleuthing revealed? The universality
of great art is a given fact, but tastes and fashions vary even for
the best. In the 1860s and 1870s when George Eliot was the delight of England, the Russians were reading her with avidity.
Later, sporadic interest paralleled the English, and has revived
with new material available in letters, biography, and criticism. If
the Russians were more reponsive to George Eliot than the French
and even the Germans,[26] that is not unusual in view of their
Anglophilia and the role of literature in Russian culture. That

the Russians read her was to be expected; how they read her might surprise those unacquainted with Russian intellectual history.

The Russian critics along with the others admired the rich, dense tapestry of life, the irony and gentle satire, the sympathetic and sensitive perception of human beings in their happiness and despair. They admired her language and its roots in the life and feelings of real people. This is an important key. Literature in Russia has often been almost a substitute for life. Art, Eliot's included, has had to satisfy deep moral and social needs, and Russian criticism has always assumed and reflected this social obligation in ways that distinguish it from European criticism.

Russia agonised in the last third of the century over the fate of the people, the *narod*. Eliot's 'domestic realism', rural settings, and social organism provided, as Gorkii implied, recognisable similarities. Russia delighted after 1850 in the scientism and attendant developments in philosophy and biology. Eliot's intellectual synthesis and biological determinism offered artistic substance for that interest. Radical Russia longed for a change in the social order. Eliot's 'meliorism' was hardly radical. Indeed, her instinct, as Russian critics noted throughout the century, was towards adjustment to present conditions or, at the most, peaceful inner transformation; yet she provided a principal component for Tkachev's theory of the professional revolutionary and her very mildness kept the censor at bay. Throughout these hundred years she has been gently chided for the narrowness of her vision, her exclusion of the larger social and political world, and her fundamental acceptance of the social arbitration of Victorian mores, of things as they are: no fighter she, for women or political and social equality.

Despite what might be called the wider insufficiencies, on balance the Russians have appreciated precisely what English-speaking readers have cherished. Special perceptions, different emphases, needs imposed by another culture, sometimes highlighted aspects less noticed at home, but the George Eliot the Russians described both in the 1860s and the 1870s is always discernible and endlessly rich.

NOTES

1 'Eliot (Marianne Evans, izv. pod psevodonimom George Eliot), Brokhaus and Efron, ed., *Entsiklopedicheskii Slovar'*, Vol. 40 (St Petersburg: 1901), pp. 647–8. U. Andreeva, 'G. Eliot v Rossii', *Problemy Angliiskoi Literatury, XIX i XX vv* (Moskva: Izd. Moskovskovo U., 1974), pp. 39–68; p. 46.

2 Ernest J. Simmons, *English Literature and Culture in Russia 1553–1840* (Cambridge, Mass.: Harvard University Press, 1935), p. 83.

3 John P. Couch, *George Eliot in France* (Chapel Hill: University of North Carolina Press, 1967), pp. 22–3. Appendix I.

4 V. G. Belinsky, 'Letter to N.V. Gogol' (3 July 1847), *Selected Philosophical Works* (Moscow: Foreign Language Pub. House, 1948), p. 509.

5 See Robert B. Bathurst, 'Dickens's Liberal Russian Readers', (unpublished dissertation, Brown University, 1977).

6 *Scenes of Clerical Life* and *Adam Bede* had two wonderful translators, according to *Vestnik Evropy* in 1884, retaining as far as possible the charm of the orginal language. *The Mill on the Floss* did not fare so well. Everything is stated, but the 'clumsiness of the phrases gives no sense of the charm of the childrens' chatter, of the particular qualities of the boy and girl, or of the delights of the majority of the scenes' A.S., 'George Eliot', *Vestnik Evropy* (1884, No. 3), p. 173.

7 Mikhail Larionovich Mikhailov was a young poet, co-author of a revolutionary proclamation of 1861 called *To the Young Generation.*

8 M.L. Mikhailov, 'Inostrannaia Literatura: George Eliot, *Adam Bede* by George Eliot, Author of *Scenes of Clerical Life*', *Sovremennik*, 78 (No. 11, 1859), 104–30; 106.

9 M. Tsebrikova, 'Anglichanki Romanistki', *Otchestvenniye Zapiski* (1871, No. 11–12. T. 199), p. 176.

10 L. K. Davydova, *George Eliot, ee zhizn' i literaturnaia deiatel'nost'* (St Petersburg: Tip. A. Tranashel, 1891), p. 80.

11 P.D. Boborykin, *Vospominaniia v dvux tomax* (SSSR, 1965), I, 488.

12 P.D. Boborykin, 'Evropeiskii Roman v 19 v,' *Romanna Zapade az dve treti veka* [The Novel in the West], (St Petersburg: 1900), pp. 347–8.

13 B.A. Kuz'min, 'Krizis angliiskovo sotsial'novo romana v 50-60x godax XIX veka'. Eliot, Trollope, Reade, Collins', *Istoriia Angliiskoi Literatury* (Moskva: Akad. Nauk, Instit. Mirovoi Literatury, 1955), XI, p. 406.

14 Quentin Anderson, *From Dickens to Hardy. Pelican Guide to English Literature*, in Gordon S. Haight, ed., *A Century of George Eliot Criticism* (Boston: Houghton Mifflin, 1965), p. 314.

15 M.L. Mikhailov, '*Novyi Roman Georga Eliota (Mill on the Floss) Sovremennik*, 83 (1860), 414.

16 Georg Lukcás, *Studies in European Realism* (London, 1950), p. 8.

17 Henry James, Review, *Nation*, New York, 3 (16 August 1866), in John Holstrom and L. Lerner, *George Eliot and her Readers* (New York, 1966), p. 73.

18 P.N. Tkachev, 'Liudi Budushchevo i Geroi Meschanstva', *Izbrannye Sochineniia* (Moskva: Izd. Vsesoiuznovo, 1932), I (1865–9), 173–234.

19 V. Ivasheva, 'Ot George Eliot k Angliiskomu romanu 60-x godov', *Voprosy Literatury*, No. 7–9 (Moskva: July 1971), p. 114.

20 Sophia Kovalevskaia, 'Vospominaniia o George Eliot', *Russkaia Mysl*, No. 6 (1886), p. 103.
21 Turgenev, I., *Polnoe Sobranie Sochineii i Pisem* (Moskva, Leningrad: Akad. Nauk, 1965), XII, #4667.
22 Tolstoi, L., *What is Art?* (trans. A. Maude) (New York: 1960), p. 152.
23 Tolstoi, L., *Polnoe Sobranie Sochineii*, 90 volumes (Moskva: 1953), 48 (11 October 1859).
24 W. C. Gareth Jones, 'George Eliot's Conception of Adam Bede and Tolstoi's Conception of Anna Karenina', *MLR*, 61 (April 1966), 473–81.
25 In a personal letter, 16 April 1980.
26 According to the *Kleines Literarisches Lexikon* (Berne, 1953) there were translations of *Adam Bede* (1860, 1887) and *The Mill on the Floss* (1861, 1890) [by Frese], *Silas Marner* (1861, 1886), *Felix Holt* [by Emil Lehmann] (1867), *Romola* (1909), *Middlemarch* (1862), *Daniel Deronda* (1918).

10   George Eliot and her Biographers

IRA BRUCE NADEL

Inscribed on the doorpost of every biographer's study might be this statement by Flaubert: 'we have too many things and not enough forms'. In epigrammatic style, it expresses the problem I want to examine in this analysis of biographical strategies and approaches adopted by various writers in their treatment of George Eliot's life. My concern is also with the formal aspects of biography, the elements of structure, narrative, and language. I begin with several general considerations of biography as a literary text.

In one sense every biography is a failure because it cannot duplicate the life of the subject nor recreate character. The myriad of facts, incidents, relationships, and settings that a biographer encounters frequently overwhelm his effort to reconstruct a life. Forced to select, balance, evaluate, and at times suppress aspects of his subject's life, the biographer is often frustrated in his attempt to unify individual experiences in an artistic manner. He must condense, eliminate, and even forget in the process of writing the life. His goal is to convey something of the personality or identity of his subject; but when this cannot be done, or when his artistic sense is thwarted by a mass of facts, he often compensates by writing an inclusive, comprehensive life that emphasises the newly gathered materials. But increasingly this traditional choice of biographical expression, the chronological and comprehensive life, is incommensurate with what we know about the complexity of individual lives. Today, new demands are placed on biography as a literary enterprise, demands resulting from developments in literary theory as much as from developments in certain genres such as the novel.

Biography is pre-eminently a narrative art, involving properties other than the mere recording of events. Bounded by fact the biographer still invents his form, directing his reader's impressions, images, and understanding of his subject through language. A helpful conceptual frame for the narrative distinctions that exist in biography is found in the division between narratives of contiguity and narratives of substitutions proposed by the French structuralist critic Todorov. Narratives of contiguity emphasise the doing or performance of events, organised in chronological order. Sequence, temporality, and causal logic shape the life which becomes the text. Narratives of substitutions accord meaning to events through repeated analysis of material presented at the beginning of the work or assumed to be understood by the reader—such as: George Eliot was a major novelist of the Victorian period whose private life involved conflict and disappointment as well as success and popularity. Narratives of substitutions structure themselves in cyclical ways with the narrative frequently turning back on itself. They concentrate on passage or transformation rather than on established states or conditions. The narrative of contiguity is linear and horizontal with history its major metaphor; the narrative of substitutions is vertical and circular with myth its major metaphor.[1]

Every biographer, no matter how objective he declares himself, interprets a life. Through his fundamental and necessary reliance on literary conventions, the biographer transforms a factual life into an aesthetic construct and makes the telling of a life as important as the details of that life.[2] In a biography referential and figurative language interact as the biographer locates a pattern or image that develops metaphorical qualities to shape the life of the subject. Indeed, for the biographer the attempt to unify the life becomes a quest for metaphor which has a dual meaning: metaphor simultaneously acts as the guiding or controlling trope of the subject's life while also embodying or projecting the biographer's conception of that life. The metaphor may either be self-generating, originating out of the life-materials or imposed by the author from his own biases. Similarly, the language of a biography provides us with clues as to how the subject envisioned him or herself. Metaphor is necessary for biography because it aids in expressing the structure of fictions promoted by the subject and allows the author to link his sense of the ideal or universal to the real and particular. Metaphor provides internal unity for the life of the subject and external unity for the author trying to fashion a text. The biographer locates coherence *in* the life and in the writing *of* the life through metaphor.

In counterpoint to these theoretical remarks is the well-rehearsed history of literary biography. With few exceptions nineteenth-century biography was a massive, monumental, personal history expressed in the well-known life and times accounts ranging from Lockhart's ten-volume *Memoirs of the Life of Sir Walter Scott* to Maitland's *The Life and Letters of Leslie Stephen*. The exceptions include Carlyle's brief *Life of John Sterling* and Gaskell's sensitive two-volume *Life of Charlotte Brontë*. The appearance of *Eminent Victorians* in 1918, shortly followed by *Queen Victoria* three years later, catapulted Lytton Strachey into the role of iconoclast who demolished the eulogistic, *res gestae* life, substituting the antagonistic, barbed but insightful life which provided judgements instead of facts, ideas instead of documents. Biography, according to received opinion, was then free to travel happily down a path cut by Freud on one side or perhaps Emil Ludwig on the other.

This standard view is in need of correction because it overlooks the pre-Stracheyean biographical revisionism demonstrated by the numerous brief lives published in serial form, represented most clearly perhaps by Samuel Smiles' multi-volumed *Lives of the Engineers* and then the English Men of Letters Series. This development of the brief life culminated in the *Dictionary of National Biography*. The received view also neglects to point out the resistance to the post-Stracheyean biographical programme of pastiche, asperity, and analysis. Biographers after Strachey largely remained conservative and empirical in their approach, dominated by such inclusive lives as W.L. Cross's three-volume *History of Henry Fielding*, Newman Ivy White's two-volume *Shelley*, Mark Schorer's *Sinclair Lewis*, or, ironically, Michael Holroyd's two-volume life of Lytton Strachey. Biography has generally abstained from the risks Strachey undertook, preferring the security of detail and documentation. This may be our defence and only resource, however, to what Leon Edel has labelled 'the age of the archive'.

Interpretation versus documentation, analysis versus the record is the persistent argument concerning the nature of biography. Evidence still outweighs ideas, however; facts still substitute for interpretation, as seen in Joseph Blotner's recent biography of

Faulkner. Yet the practitioners who permit themselves to theorise still argue for some ideal interpretive life, as Richard Ellmann stated in his otherwise conservative analysis entitled 'Literary Biography'. 'More than anything else we want in modern biography to see the character forming, its peculiarites taking shape,' he wrote. Biography will continue to be dominated by fact, Ellmann asserts; but almost unwillingly he admits that 'the best ones will offer speculations, conjectures, hypotheses'.[3]

For George Eliot the numerous biographical approaches applied to her life — there have been roughly twenty-two book-length accounts — significantly parallel the troubled history and theory of biography and indicate the effort of the biographer, especially in recent times, to locate a form appropriate to his subject. An early example is the minor English poetess Mathilde Blind's life, *George Eliot*, published in London by W.H. Allen in 1883. It appeared in the Eminent Women Series edited by John H. Ingram and marks the influence of the serial life, the introductory record following a specific format. Blind's approach anticipates the volume by Leslie Stephen in the English Men of Letters Series. The author of *The Prophecy of Saint Oran and Other Poems*, Blind (a writer the *Athenaeum* praised as being one of 'the few contemporary poets who could have done so much dramatic business in so few lines'[4]) attempts to be thorough and accurate. Like John Walter Cross, Blind cites the aid of Mr Isaac Evans in addition to Mr and Mrs Charles Bray, Miss Sara Hennell, and 'contemporaries of . . . Mr. Robert Evans' (p. iii). Previously unpublished letters coupled with an emphasis on the feminist accomplishments of Eliot give the biography a detailed and distinctive outlook. One of its distinctions is that it provides, for the first time, the correct birthplace and date of Mary Ann Evans. [But *Coton* is misspelt *Colton*. Ed.] The enthusiasm of Blind, however, fashions numerous overstatements such as that George Eliot is 'the greatest realist . . . of her sex', in contrast to George Sand who is 'the greatest idealist of her sex' (p. 6), or that Eliot combines in extraordinary ways intellectual power and 'an unparalleled vision for the homely details of life' (p. 5). Although limited by a lack of extensive data, Blind's well-researched book shows that the uniform and uneventful life of Eliot was a myth in contrast to early memorial accounts of her life shortly after her death.[5] By contrast, Blind suggests a stressful, troubled existence for George Eliot but one that had a heroic if not transcendent quality.

John Walter Cross's three-volume life of Eliot appeared two years after Blind's and of course for many years remained the standard life. In contrast to his predecessor, Cross knew the subject intimately yet strove to preserve a distance between his role as biographer and his subject. This resulted, of course, in the well-known truncation of the letters, the resistance to comment on various events in the life and a general avoidance of conclusions. But Cross conceived of his life as an *'autobiography'* of Eliot as he announced in the opening sentence, and it may be unfair to judge his work exclusively as a biography.[6] With its prejudicial and protective attitude, Cross's life remains a memorial to Victorian biographical practice with its emphasis on letters to tell the story, its chronological, day-to-day narrative structure, and its stress on accuracy ('everything depends on accuracy' he wrote [p. vi]).

The detail, arrangement, and precision of Cross's life of Eliot anticipate the very shape of Gordon Haight's biography eighty-three years later. Cross's life, in fact, sets a pattern that Eliot's most authoritative biographer has followed. Both stress the daily life, liberally quote from the letters which are similarly the principal source of information, and both resist interpretation of the life and the literature. In addition, Cross and Haight deal extensively with sources, emphasise Eliot's sensitivity to criticism as well as her diffident behaviour, and concentrate on 'the development of her intellect and character' (p. v). They drastically differ, of course, in the full disclosure of facts and complete citation of material found in Haight and absent in Cross. Joining a series of Victorian widow or widower biographers such as Mrs Kingsley or Mrs Clough, Cross's life stands as an example of the Victorian passion for remembrance, protection, and selective accuracy.

'No flowers by request' was the unofficial motto of the *Dictionary of National Biography*, and Leslie Stephen in his 1902 life of George Eliot in the English Men of Letters Series clearly follows the principle. Author of an earlier, 1881 tribute to Eliot in the *Cornhill*, Stephen was eminently suited to deal with her life and work. Like Cross, he favoured the use of letters in telling the life, but he also recognised the need to condense: 'To write a life is to collect the particular heap of rubbish in which his [the biographer's] material is contained, to sift the relevant from the superincumbent mass and then try to smelt it and cast it into its natural mold'. In another passage from this same essay on biography, Stephen anticipates Strachey, as well as his own life of

Eliot, when he writes 'we have to learn the art of forgetting—of suppressing all the multitudinous details which threaten to overburden the human memory. Our aim should be to present the human soul, not all its irrelevant bodily trappings'.[7]

The desire to condense, however, overrides the possibility of conveying a soul in Stephen's life to Eliot. The style is abrupt, rigid, and cold, as in this comment on Eliot's sense of duty expressed in a letter while she stayed in Geneva in 1850. Says Stephen: 'The phrase is significant. She was now thirty years old, and her outlook was sufficiently vague. She had grown to her full intellectual stature. She had read widely and intelligently'.[8] More directly than either Blind or Cross, however, Stephen provides a criticism of Eliot's literary works and indulges in some theorising about literature as in his comment on subjectivism in fiction in relation to *The Mill on the Floss* or on morality in literature (pp. 87–8, 117). He is also unafraid to criticise her characters, calling Stephen Guest, for example, 'a mere hairdresser's block' (p. 104). Stephen also marks his debt to earlier biographies of Eliot, notably Blind (pp. 105–6). A healthy contextualism emerges in the life so that we see Eliot in European framework, especially in relation to French nineteenth-century writing (p. 111). Overall, a welcomed irreverence appears in Stephen's life, refreshingly engaging for the reader and author alike.

Stephen's account, an extension of the critical tone and approach found in the *DNB*, is a reaction to the adulation expressed by Cross. A sensitivity of response challenges the narrative which involves the reader in the biographer's unfolding estimate of his subject. This sense of the puzzle and confusions of the life and their recognition as such by the biographer who, in turn, avoids pre-disposed or pre-formulated opinions characterises some of the most recent suggestions about biographical writing as Robert Gittings has noted.[9] Although Stephen, writing the biography late in his life—he died within two years—appears distant from his subject, partly because he had little sympathy with fiction, the book is a healthy critique of Eliot's life and career, an antidote to the uncritical and voluminous life Cross compiled. The value of her novels, Stephen concludes, again anticipating several more recent biographers, is that they are 'implicit autobiography' and manifest a sympathetic nature united with 'a large and tolerant intellect' (p. 201). The scepticism of Stephen, particularly when dealing with the philosophic aspects of Eliot's work, is in part a re-

action against what he felt to be idolising tendencies in her reputation. His biography is a corrective, limited but honest in its
appraisal; it may be thought of as the first critical biography of
Eliot and her work.

The Freudian domination of biography lasted roughly from
1920 to 1935 and might be epitomised by Lewis Mumford's 1929
life of Herman Melville. The psychic significance of ordinary and
extraordinary events were consistently analysed as the unconscious, repressed, sublimated, or compulsive aspects of human
behaviour and compelled the biographer to speculate and inter-
pret. Anne Fremantle's life of Eliot in the 'Great Lives' series,
published by Duckworth in 1933, illustrates many of these pre-
occupations. De-emphasising the early life and religious conflict
(to be stressed by Haight and then Ruby Redinger), Fremantle
concentrates on London, *The Westminster Review* and tangen-
tially the literary works of Eliot. It is perhaps the first biography
to make use of the diaries of John Chapman. Context, however,
merges with psychological overstatement to produce a biography that has as its theme the interaction of retribution and
tradition.

Unlike Stephen's discrete and even unconnected remarks,
Fremantle's account is unified by her themes. There is also
greater candour in detailing the emotional life of Eliot, in contrast to the objective assessment of Stephen. Of Lewes's commitment to Marian Evans, for example, Fremantle writes that 'there
was a great risk that he might quickly tire of the ponderous,
middle-aged, priggish and high minded but humorless woman
who was giving up everything for him'.[10] This 'storm-tried
matron', however, is subject to excessive speculative analysis in a
neo-Freudian manner. We are told, for example, that Griff was
Marian's secret garden, or that the real reason for Hetty's punish-
ment was that 'Marian's whole creed, first as an Evangelical, then
as a disciple of Mr. Bray's, later still as a Positivist, was that the
wages of sin are paid C.O.D.; her whole philosophy was a
spiritual accepting of absolutely inevitable consequences' (p. 87).
This law of consequence, of guilt, Fremantle proposes as the key
to understanding the action of Eliot and her heroines: 'As, when a
child, she had driven into her wooden doll's head the nails her
wicked aunts should have endured, so now she made her books
what her dolls had once been: the sublimation of her vision of
retributive justice' (p. 88).

Near the end of her account, Fremantle tells us that Eliot suffered from a 'deepening earnestness of gloom' but that her marriage to Cross was her attainment of at least tradition and the entry
into a world of 'regularity' (pp. 100, 136). Anticipating a later
and better argued case by Ruby Redinger, Fremantle avoids
evidence or detail in her assertions. In her enthusiasm for psychological interpretation, she overstates her position. Reflecting the
absorption with the psychological that highlighted biographical
writing in the thirties, Fremantle paradoxically simplifies the life
of Eliot while overinterpreting it. A curious counter-reaction
merges within the biography so that the moral psychology of Eliot
is found to be antithetical to the Freudian concerns of the day:
'her psychology', writes Fremantle, 'is abhorrent to our psycho-
analytical generation' (p. 140). We are also told that Eliot 'had no
sense of form, and no love of, nor gift for handling, words' (p.
142). But admirably for Fremantle, George Eliot was a rebel,
reacting against the inhibiting conventions of Victorian life while
providing 'invaluable guides to the Victorian attitude of mind' (p.
141). Distrustful of Victorian earnestness, supportive of psychological interpretation, Fremantle's opinionated life stimulates our
impression of Eliot by its directness, suggestion of human foibles
and presentation of weaknesses.

To counter the prejudices and errors of earlier lives and to in-
corporate his own magisterial scholarship, Gordon Haight
published his biography of George Eliot in 1968. It immediately
superseded all others. A work of outstanding research, it nonetheless might be seen as the apotheosis of the scholarly, academic
biography in dramatic contrast, both in form and substance, to a
biography that appeared the following year: Erik Erikson's
Gandhi's Truth. From the perspective of the evolving form of
modern biographical writing, the two works stand in absolute
opposition to one another, the former displaying the best of the
academic approach, the latter exhibiting the new direction of
psycho-biography that has characterised a great deal of recent
work. For Haight it is the accumulation of evidence that determines his form, establishing a narrative of continuity; for
Erikson, it is the identity of significant configurations in a life
fusing it into a whole that determines his form, or narrative of
substitutions.

George Eliot: A Biography by Gordon Haight reflects a stage in
the writing of literary lives by academics. These lives are meticul-

ous in their detail and scrupulous in their documentation. They also, however, tend to avoid any analysis of the writer's work, fail to establish any theoretical connections between individual experience and the literary text and concentrate on influence rather than interpretation. Other lives that appeared in the sixties which exhibit these qualities include Mark Schorer's *Sinclair Lewis* (1961), Herschel Baker's *Hazlitt* (1962), Arthur and Barbara Gelb's *O'Neill* (1962), William Riley Parker's *Milton* (1966), R.W. Stallman's *Stephen Crane* (1968), and Carlos Baker's *Hemingway* (1969). These biographies are inclusive, archival and comprehensive in detail, acting as records rather than responses to the life. A minor example of the contrast between this approach and, say, Erikson's is the absence of any statement about method at the beginning of Haight's life of Eliot and the several pages devoted to procedure in Erikson's life of Gandhi. While Haight's life of Eliot remains an outstanding contribution to Eliot scholarship, it is nonetheless unadventurous and conservative in approach like a large number of scholarly biographies in the sixties.

More particularly, Haight is hesitant to judge. This clearly balances the excesses of the Fremantle approach but still disappoints the expectations of a reader. '[S]peculations are futile; one can tell only the facts', Haight announces on page 22, yet his account of important events in the life of Eliot demands interpretation.[11] Haight's sympathies lie elsewhere and he patronises those 'Freudians' who might elaborate, for example, the meaning of Marian Evans's forgetting her brooch containing a lock of her father's hair in her haste to return to London from Rosehill to meet Lewes (p. 135).

Fact alone cannot determine a life nor can it fashion a narrative. In his account of Eliot, Haight provides a surfeit of fact, reaching such lengths as to name the mountains Herbert Spencer climbed in a summer 1853 tour of Switzerland or to specify the precise dates John Chapman went to bed with his mistress Elisabeth Tilley (pp. 118, 87, 93). This concern with detail derives from an attachment to letters to tell the story for Haight but also illustrates the influence or effect of a biographer's subject upon the text. The paramount place of domestic detail in the fiction of Eliot appears to be echoed in Haight's accumulation of important domestic facts.

In his lengthy life of Eliot, Haight offers only tenuous interpretations of events and none of the work (see pp. 52, 79, 86). He shies away from analysis and confuses the issue, as when in a single sentence censuring the John Chapman relationship, he momentarily presents a theory but then rejects it. After quoting from Chapman's diary, Haight writes

> There can be little doubt that Marian was guilty of some indiscretion, probably more serious than holding hands. Her over-ready expansiveness, her incapability of practising the required conventionalism, her unfortunately balanced moral and animal regions — all come to mind (p. 86).

But interpretive reticence replaces the anticipated conclusion. The passage shifts suddenly to Chapman's reputation as a philanderer, Marian's susceptibility to affection, and the detail of Chapman relating to a friend in the 1890s that Eliot was once very fond of him. Haight's tone is defensive, but his innuendos are troublesome and the absence of a knowledgeable interpretation is dangerously left to the reader. A suppressed hostility to psychologising about her life appears throughout the biography.

Acting to unite the facts, however, is a muted metaphor found in the repeated references to George Eliot's need for someone to lean on. Haight first refers to this when citing a passage from Charles Bray's *Autobiography* dealing with George Combe's analysis of Eliot's phrenological cast made in 1842. Chapter vi in the biography borrows the image for its title. Most interestingly, Haight first employed this image in 1940 in his study *George Eliot and John Chapman*. There, Haight declared:

> In that phrase lies the key to an understanding of that extraordinary life. All the strange contradictions in her career from the passionate childhood dependence on her brother... to her marriage with John W. Cross a few months before her death are explained by her 'always requiring some one to lean on'.[12]

In the 1968 biography Haight applies the same 'key', only enlarging its application to the entire life. Conceptually, Haight's earliest perception of Eliot's life remained unchanged between 1940 and 1968 and one might ungenerously remark that in this approach to Eliot we have the only major biographical study of a nineteenth-century writer with its interpretive foundation em-

bedded in phrenology. Furthermore, the determinancy of fact in
the narrative structure and language of the biography has de-
valued the application of other figurative language in the life and
made insufficent use of the posturing image for analysing or har-
monising the life. Additional difficulties in the biography include
the minimal sense of prolepsis as the life-narrative unfolds and
the absence of any sense of Eliot's development as a writer. The
singular, and let me emphasise, significant accomplishment of
the biography is the establishment of the record, but the result is
ultimately unsatisfying because a series of crucial questions
concerning personality and creative development remain after we
have completed a reading of the book.

In part a response to this factual life and in part a desire to present an integrated life-account, Ruby Redinger published *George
Eliot: The Emergent Self* in 1975. Supplementing these reasons
and explaining a great deal of the importance of Redinger's work
is an awareness in the text of the difficulty of writing biography.
The work is an example of psycho-biography, equivalent in
nature to two other biographies published the same year: Bruce
Mazlish's *James and John Stuart Mill, Father and Son in the 19th
Century* and Karl Miller's *Cockburn's Millennium*, a biography of
the Scottish jurist and writer Henry Cockburn. What these works
have in common is a concern with a fundamental portrait of the
subject's inner world, organised around either significant
moments in that life or probing questions concerning that life.
For Redinger, the central issue is why did Eliot begin to write
creatively only in middle-age? The very centre of her biography is
the formation of the imaginative life of the subject, the essential
interest in the life of any artist. Psycho-biography attempts to see
the life of the subject in its totality discovering or inventing 'the
organic unity that links all the aspects of his [the subject's] life together'.[13] By definition and intent, this form of biography demands interpretation, originality and analysis. Redinger accepts
this challenge and creates what is to date our most imaginative
life of Eliot.

Redinger's biography exhibits Todorov's narrative as substitutions theory, refreshingly adhering to no rigid chronological
structure. It begins with a sympathetic analysis of Cross's biography and the context in which it was completed. The biography then becomes a kind of Freudian 'family romance' but
without the doctrinaire emphases a Freudian would impose. Its

structure is proleptic, forming an advancing spiral that thrusts characters and events forward and then returns to an original point until the next thrust. This 'cyclical construction of substitutions', as Todorov might call it, provides an involving narrative that unites moment and sequence. But in her pursuit of a psychological interpretation, Redinger is fully aware of its dangers: 'psychic phenomena', she writes, 'defy verbal descripion; if it is attempted, the results are usually misleading'.[14] However, Redinger disproves her own indictment.

Focusing on the shaping events of George Eliot's imagination, notably her childhood, adolescence, and young womanhood, Redinger stresses the idea of emergence. She repeatedly demonstrates the unity between early events and later actions. Concentrating on family conflicts (especially George Eliot's alienation from her mother), as well as Eliot's self-doubts and the early association between the imagination, day-dreaming, and guilt, Redinger explores the elements that alternately prevented George Eliot from writing creatively until 1857 and yet provided her with the materials for her fictions. This, the very substance of Redinger's biography, is limitedly treated in Haight's account (cf. pp. 205–7) of her life. Moreover, the elaboration of a comment Eliot made to Sara Hennell in 1844 on childhood is the creative source of Redinger's entire work: 'Childhood is only the beautiful and happy time in contemplation and retrospect — to the child it is full of deep sorrows, the meaning of which is unknown' (p. 50). To define that meaning and clarify its significance is Redinger's goal.

Strikingly free from psychological jargon, Redinger nonetheless is unafraid to psychologise about the progress of Eliot as a writer. Summarising her hesitancy to write yet possession of an intense imagination, Redinger explains that

> Had her imagination not held an autonomous position in her ego but functioned primarily as a defense against the various threats to her ego, it would have flourished during her unhappiest years and collapsed when she regained happiness and emotional security. Fortunately, her strongest defenses were against imagination itself, so that when they were broken down, it was at last free, and she was to be at her most creative during her happiest years (p. 53).

Associating Eliot's Evangelicalism with her prose style, Redinger provides an original approach to understanding the novels. Her balanced and lengthy sentences, she suggests, were ways to conceal certain aggressive tendencies and protect 'the pith of their content' from hostile readers (pp. 78–9). Throughout the biography Redinger provides psychologically condensed explanations of Eliot's life (see pp. 286, 288–9); and in an effort to establish the identity of Eliot as a writer, she presents venturesome theories, imaginative interpretations and bold assertions.

Of course, Redinger is not without faults and they include an excess of speculation, a compressed criticism of the fiction, and a desire for psychological certainty that leads, for example, to the suggestion that 20 September 1850, the death of Latimer in 'The Lifted Veil', is also the birthday of Eliot's 'life of creativity' (p. 401). The biography also has a truncated ending and an undue emphasis on the financial arrangements, publishing disputes and reaction of reviewers to Eliot's novels. Nonetheless, Redinger synthesises ideas, clearly supports her opinions, unabashedly assesses previous lives, experiments with structure, and seeks to understand, as immediately as possible, the importance of the subject's life. For Redinger, Eliot is an active not passive individual, one who 'occasionally has annoyed or disturbed me but has never bored me' (p. x).

One finishes *George Eliot: The Emergent Self* with a sense of knowing something of Eliot as a person. The conjecture, psychologising, and structure contribute to a dynamic narrative that involves the reader in the unfolding of the imaginative and psychological life of the subject. It satisfies our need to understand the pattern of creativity and thought beyond the record of events and allows the reader to participate in the actual events that become the substance of Eliot's fictions.

By concentrating on the major versions of the life of George Eliot I have by necessity had to avoid a series of other lives, notably dual biographies such as Anna T. Kitchel's *George Lewes and George Eliot: A Review of Records* (1933), Gordon Haight's previously mentioned *George Eliot and John Chapman* (1940), and K. A. McKenzie's *Edith Simcox and George Eliot* (1961). There are also additional approaches such as Mary H. Deakins' *The Early Life of George Eliot* (1913), and Pierre Bourl'honne's intellectual biography (1933). The same year as Haight's bio-

graphy appeared Rosemary Sprague published a popularised life
that substituted explication of the novels for analysis of the life.
F.W. Kenyon's *The Consuming Flame: The Story of George Eliot*
appeared in 1970 as an example of a recent fictionalised account
of her life, an imitation of Emilie and Georges Romieu's French
fictionalisation, *La Vie de George Eliot* (1930; tr. Brian W.
Downs and published by Dutton in 1932).

From a survey of the major lives, however, one becomes more
conscious of the problems of biographical expression, but like the
frustrated biographer I characterised at the beginning, one becomes more disheartened at the thought of providing a single,
workable conclusion incorporating the varied approaches displayed by the various biographies of George Eliot. Nonetheless,
when a biographer recognises that the life he writes is itself an
aesthetic construct involving fictions, imagery, style, and narra-
tion, parallel to the inner life of his subject, itself a fiction, the
result may be a life that is at the same time literary and truthful.
It will also reflect the ambiguous, self-contradictory, illogical individual that is its subject. Redinger's life comes closest to this
ideal through its sense of discovery and evaluation that involves
the reader as well as the biographer. Every biography is of course
incomplete, but Redinger comes nearest to the goal George Eliot
herself outlined in a letter to Mrs. Gaskell about her biography of
Charlotte Brontë. 'It makes us', she wrote,

> familiar inmates of an interior so strange, so original in its
> individual elements and so picturesque in its externals—it
> paints for us at once the psychological drama and the scenic
> accessories with so much vividness—that fiction has nothing
> more wild, touching and heart-strengthing to place above it.[15]

In this sense Redinger has co-ordinated the biographical form
with the life-record to discern, in the words of Leon Edel, 'the
complexities of being without pretending that life's riddles have
been answered'.[16]

NOTES

1   Tzvetan Todorov, *The Poetics of Prose*, tr. Richard Howard (1971; Ithaca:
     Cornell University Press, 1977), p. 135.
2   See Susan Sontag where she argues that 'the knowledge we gain through art

is an experience of the form or style of knowing something, rather than a knowledge of something (like a fact or a moral judgment) in itself', *Against Interpretation* (New York: Dell, 1969), p. 30. It is also helpful to remember Jakobson's dictum: 'The object of literary study is not literature but literariness, that is, what makes a given work a literary work', Jakobson in Todorov, *The Poetics of Prose*, p. 248.

3 Richard Ellmann, 'Literary Biography', *Golden Codgers: Biographical Speculations* (New York: Oxford University Press, 1973), p. 15.

4 Mathilde Blind, *George Eliot* (London: W.H. Allen, 1883), endpaper [p. 219]. All further references are to this edition.

5 See for example the account in *Blackwoods*, 129 (February 1881), 255–68.

6 John Walter Cross, *George Eliot's Life as Related in Her Letters and Journals, New Edition* (Edinburgh: Blackwood, 1885), p. v. All further references are to this edition.

7 Leslie Stephen, 'Biography', *Men, Books, and Mountains, Essays by Leslie Stephen*, introd. S.O.A. Ullmann (London: Hogarth Press, 1956), pp. 132, 140–1. The essay originally appeared in the *National Review*, 22 (1893).

8 Leslie Stephen, *George Eliot* (London: Macmillan, 1902; rpt. New York: AMS Press, 1973), p. 36. All further references are to this edition.

9 Robert Gittings, *The Nature of Biography* (Seattle: University of Washington Press, 1978), *passim*.

10 Anne Fremantle, *George Eliot* (London: Duckworth, 1933), p. 65. All further references are to this edition. [Text reads 'storm-tried', p. 77. Ed.]

11 Gordon S. Haight, *George Eliot: A Biography* (Oxford: Clarendon Press, 1968), p. 22. All further references are to this edition.

12 Gordon S. Haight, *George Eliot and John Chapman*, 2nd edn. (1940; New Haven: Archon Books, 1969), p. vii.

13 Jerrold Seigel, *Marx's Fate, The Shape of A Life* (Princeton: Princeton University Press, 1978), p. 4.

14 Ruby V. Redinger, *George Eliot: The Emergent Self* (New York: Alfred A. Knopf, 1975), p. 126. All further references are to this edition.

15 George Eliot, *The George Eliot Letters*, ed. Gordon S. Haight, 9 vols (New Haven: Yale University Press, 1954–78), ii, 315.

16 Leon Edel, 'The Poetics of Biography', *Contemporary Approaches to English Studies*, ed. Hilda Schiff (London: Heinemann, 1977), p. 42.

11   The Ambivalence of *The Mill on the Floss*

IAN ADAM

'So intensely real is it that I am not sure whether I did not exclaim aloud 'Why the devil is she putting poor Maggie into a position where she would be more than human if she did not come to grief".'[1]

The Mill on the Floss (1860) is perhaps the most troubled of its author's novels. We may praise the sharpness of its presentation of place and person, its evocation of childhood incident and experience, its humour and satire, the fascination of its heroine or its study of community in terms which suggest a creation triumphantly achieved, and yet accompany such remarks with reservations, more often uneasily than definitively asserted, about the objects of our praise. The history of the criticism reveals many such recurrent questions, which in summary tend to take an antinomical form. Is the final flood a *deus ex machina*, or an event artistically conceived and executed? Is our final attitude towards the Dodsons to be one of praise or blame? How do we reconcile the Wordsworthian elevation of the past with the satiric observations made on it? The evocation of a childhood idyll with its manifest sorrows? Is Maggie a developing character, or a neurotic, condemned to repeat the mistakes of the past? Is she demonic or dutiful? Does the work affirm or deny the authority of convention?

These have been and continue to be controversial questions, and perhaps they are finally unresolvable. For I want to suggest that they arise less because one reader or another on either side of any question has exhibited shrewdness or obtuseness than because the author has so rendered her material as to make such incompatible readings possible. The criticism persistently shows a mixed response which accurately reflects the author's own uncertainties. In arguing this thesis I am inevitably going to be drawn into questions which go beyond the identification and description of these uncertainties to their sources and origins.

Many of the issues raised by the novel are concerned with its heroine, Maggie Tulliver, whose confusions few readers will deny. It follows that I must argue some kind of implication of the author in these, for I cannot with consistency assert her uneasy handling of her material and exempt from that thesis a major portion of it. The relation of character to creator is always complex, and in this case, with its many autobiographical elements, perhaps specially so. One working distinction I am going to make immediately is that between Maggie as a character whose confusions are *locally* understood or 'placed', and Maggie as one whose *broad destiny* reveals the author's inability finally to come to terms with them.

I take as my central text a scene which is epitomic of many issues in the novel. It takes place on Maggie's second visit to her brother at Mr Stelling's school. In it she silently watches Tom and Philip at their studies.

In the afternoon the boys were at their books in the study, preparing the morrow's lessons, that they might have a holiday in the evening in honour of Maggie's arrival. Tom was hanging over his Latin grammar, moving his lips inaudibly like a strict but impatient Catholic repeating his tale of paternosters; and Philip, at the other end of the room, was busy with two volumes, with a look of contented diligence that excited Maggie's curiosity; he did not look at all as if he were learning a lesson. She sat on a low stool at nearly a right angle with the two boys, watching first one and then the other, and Philip, looking off his book once towards the fireplace, caught the pair of questioning dark eyes fixed upon him. He thought this sister of Tulliver's seemed a nice little thing, quite unlike her brother; he wished *he* had a little sister. What was it, he wondered, that made Maggie's dark eyes remind him of the stories about princesses being turned into animals? . . . . . . I think it was that her eyes were full of unsatisfied intelligence, and unsatisfied, beseeching affection.[2]

First of all Maggie is at the centre of this scene. She is physically placed at the centre, at a virtual right angle to the two boys: it is her dark eyes, watching first one, then the other, which dominate. This positioning, those dominant eyes, are metonymic of her psychic and thematic centrality in the novel. Second, that alternating glance suggests the deliberations which lead to choice, the weighing of alternatives, and Maggie's choices are to be central to its action. Third, Philip's wish that he had a little sister, a wish prompted by thoughts of Maggie, introduces a theme the novel is to explore, her relations with Tom, her biological brother, and Philip, with whom she feels an affinity in spirit. Fourth, the objects of her regard, those opposing personalities Tom and Philip, suggest qualities and values prominent in the work: the known and the exotically unknown, the practical and the bookish, the methodical and the imaginative. Finally Philip's identification of her with one of those 'princesses . . . turned into animals', a linking immediately endorsed by the author, expresses in a brief mythic allusion her condition for much of the novel. Maggie, in summary, is central, striving towards choice, doubly committed, and somehow denied her true nature.

That Maggie is central in the novel few would debate, but it is worth examining the sense in which this is so. She does not represent some kind of Jamesian consciousness to which all its elements are subordinate. She is intelligent, but not a 'fine central intelligence' through whose awareness is filtered the major significance of the action. Rather, the novelist is committed to multiple perspectives. In the early part of the book, for example, Mr Tulliver's viewpoint dominates many scenes, and elsewhere it may be Tom's or, as briefly in the above quotation, Philip's. Parts of the novel, such as Tom's experiences at school, have only a marginal relation to Maggie's history, while in others, such as the story of the downfall of the house of Tulliver, the focus is on the family, of which Maggie is an important rather than the only significant member. And even later in the work, when the concern is more exclusively with Maggie, the author will divert our attention from her for such a lively 'free' chapter as that in which Bob Jakin entertains us in teaching Mrs Glegg the breadth of his thumb (v, 2: 269–84).

We may see this relative subordination of the heroine as a formal choice. The novel is stubbornly Victorian, with a slacker commitment to unity than modern fiction, or, if we like, with a commitment to a different kind of unity, one which is conceived as residing in the vision of author rather than character. But there is, as well, an ethical dimension to the narrative form. One of the lessons which Maggie learns, again and again, is that the needs and desires of her being cannot be satisfied without consideration of the needs and desires of others. The author cannot with consistency assert this ethic without creating the autonomous consciousnesses of these others, without giving them a place in the sun. Maggie is to learn to subdue the self; the reader perceives a novel in which form quietly underlines the need for its subordination. But it is obvious that both the author through formal choice and the character through ethical choice must strike a balance. Maggie's diminishment must stop short well this side of her annihilation; the end of her egoism must not be the assumption of tyranny by others over her. Maggie, who alternates between extremes of self-sacrifice and self-indulgence, has difficulty finding that balance; the novelist handles the formal placing with a sure, not to say masterful touch. Nevertheless there is some evidence that she alters her conception of the prominence due her heroine towards the novel's end. To this point I shall return.

Maggie's oscillating glances suggest the deliberations which lead to choice. All novelists must dramatise choice in some way or another — how else could they account for human action? — but George Eliot is unusual in the stress she gives to its philosophic, ethical and psychological dimensions. As George Levine's classic essay, 'Determinism and Responsibility in George Eliot'[3] and many passages in the novels demonstrate, she was very preoccupied with the vexatious question of human free will; as her early essay on 'The Antigone and its Moral'[4] and many situations in the novels show, she was fascinated by characters who face contending ethical claims; and, as her entire *oeuvre* reveals, she frequently writes with her highest powers most fully engaged when considering the interaction of thought and feeling at times of decision. Thought corrupted by feeling; thought denying legitimacy to feeling; feeling and thought in harmony; feeling responding to human need without intercession of 'any irritable reaching after fact and reason': examples from the stories of Tito, or Esther Lyon, or Dorothea or Gwendolen could easily overwhelm us in application. *The Mill on the Floss* is like the other novels in providing instances of the author's persistent preoccupation with choice, but unusual in its presentation of ultimate indecisiveness. Maggie's glances do not finally settle on Tom or Philip but oscillate between them in strong attachment to one and attraction to the other. The novel here as elsewhere asserts a see-saw nature. In explicit comment we have many such references as those to her 'passions at war' (I, 10: 90), or a 'daring' followed by 'timidity', (I, 11: 96) or to a 'sense of opposing elements, of which a fierce collision is imminent' (V, 1: 261). Behaviourally we see her batter her doll-fetish against a wall, and then make-believe to poultice it, or alternate between rebellious fantasy and dutiful resignation in reaction to the family downfall. She acts, and then retracts. In three major episodes in the work, often linked for their psychological symmetry, there is the same pattern. She determines to leave home and run away to the gypsies, only to change her mind when she discovers they do not fit her romantic preconception of them. She ardently embraces renunciation, and then evades it in secret meetings with Philip in the Red Deeps. She is carried away by her passion for Stephen, and then renounces him; feels renewed temptation on the receipt of his letter, and then renounces him again by burning it. Such sequences of contradictory commitments, as Barbara Hardy has pointed out, give the novel a moral movement unique in the fiction, closer to eddying or oscillation than progression.[5]

Principles informing this fluctuating pattern of action seem to emerge from the examples cited. The fluctuation appears less one between overriding and contrary passions (though it is sometimes that) than one between overriding passion and its denial, between strong feeling and guilt at its expression. And while we may relate this definition of pattern to that image of Maggie caught between Tom and Philip, there are some difficulties with the model. Tom from beginning to end of the novel rebukes Maggie for what he sees as her irresponsible impulsiveness and indeed represents that voice of duty which compels guilt. But Philip, with his decency and kindness, hardly seems an emblem of the energy of powerful feeling. When we think of that in the novel we immediately think of Maggie's father. Tom, of course, has the Dodson character, and the attitudes to feeling between which Maggie fluctuates seem to be those represented by the contrasting temperaments of her brother and father, Dodson and Tulliver. Nevertheless there is an important point of contact with Philip, which should emerge in discussion.

The Dodsons have virtually starved feelings into submission. Among the fixities of preoccupation with impeccable wills, do-

mestic economies, pills and potions, the tight rolling of table
napkins, the dangers of draughts, 'the thorough scouring of
wooden and copper utensils', and the failings of neighbours,
there is little room for their play. The 'hereditary custom' of
family ritual, sufficient unto itself, keeps order as firmly as the
locked doors in Mrs Pullet's house keep rooms and wardrobes un-
contaminated by human use. Mr Tulliver is also governed by
'traditional belief', but it is carried in 'richer blood', which races
at real or imagined offence, causing the blind charge on issues of
principle, in disregard of facts or consequences (IV, 1: 238–40, *et
passim*). Gentlemen can deal with foxy lawyers; therefore the
practical Tom must have an impractical gentleman's education.
Mrs Glegg and Mr Tulliver quarrel at dinner; therefore her loan
of £500 must be forthwith returned. Mr Pivart's plans for
irrigation upstream from Dorlcote constitute a violation of water
rights; therefore a lawsuit must be launched. It is no wonder that
Tulliver and Dodson clash. One has passion clouding his sense of
reality, while the other's sense of reality neuters his passion. And
the plight of Maggie's feeling life is that she finds difficulty in
achieving a middle way between such famine and feast.

Both Dodson and Tulliver lack a sense of proportion, but one
finds itself more easily accommodated into the society of the novel
than the other. The short-sighted, mercantile citizens of St Ogg's
are not much out of step with Dodson values (though we should
not overlook the author's emphasis on some uniquely Dodson
forms of integrity). Mr Tulliver, both in weaknesses and
strengths, is linked less with the town as it is than as it was. He
may be unconscious of history, but it lives in him. In his capacity
for belief in the absolute rightness of his cause he is linked with its
period of civil wars and religious martyrdom, 'where first Puritans
thanked God for the blood of the Loyalists, and then Loyalists
thanked God for the blood of the Puritans' (I, 12: 105). But in
gentler moods he is also linked with the town's legendary
boatman, Ogg, whose moving story, recorded in Book I, Chapter
12, tells of human need, a flood, and compassion, and ironically
comments on the novel's final chapters.[6] We think of Ogg in
connection with many tender touches on Mr Tulliver's part: his
kind treatment of Maggie on her return from her adventure with
the gypsies, for example, or his change of heart about calling in
his loan of £300 to Mr Moss, his financially distressed brother-in-
law (I, 8: 75–6). Such capacity for sympathetic imagination

represented for George Eliot a way of dealing with the passions, their civilisation. She wrote to John Sibree in February, 1848: 'The passions and senses decompose, so to speak. The intellect by its analytic power, restrains the fury with which they rush to their own destruction, the moral nature purifies, beautifies and at length transmutes them' (*Letters*, I, 251). Mr Tulliver does not have the 'analytic power' to entirely 'restrain' their 'fury', but he does have the 'moral nature' which allows him at times to 'transmute' them. And that capacity is linked with cultural inheritance in local myth which, sadly, most of St Ogg's seems to ignore.

This side to Mr Tulliver provides a mediatory and conciliatory model of behaviour for Maggie. And its potential is reinforced when we consider that it is a similar capacity for compassion and understanding that we find in Philip, and that some of Maggie's attraction to him undoubtedly lies in her intimation of this. She glances at someone who has qualities of her Tulliver father that her biological brother lacks. 'Why do you like my eyes?' she asks when he says he wishes he had a sister with dark eyes, just like hers, and she reflects that she 'had never heard any one but her father speak of her eyes as if they had merit' (II, 6: 164). It is mainly Philip, from feelings obviously more than fraternal, who is to insist on the brotherly relation, but ironically for him, his role for her becomes just that. 'What a dear, good brother you would have been, Philip', she declares at one of their meetings in the Red Deeps, contrasting him with Tom, . . . 'You would have loved me well enough to bear with me, and forgive me everything' (V, 3: 287). He becomes for her the Tom who should have been: patient, sympathetic, and constant, bound to her by affection having 'its root deep down in her childhood' (VI, 7: 359).

Philip, like Maggie's father, provides her with the sympathetic affection she craves, but he also provides another kind of nourishment. In quality his cultural inheritance is like that of her father at its best, but in substance it is both broader in origins and more conscious in expression. In addition to suggesting a civilising capacity to form, without suppressing, the energy of human feeling, it also suggests a source for that capacity outside of local community, and hence an alternative to it. When Maggie glances at Tom and Philip she glances at a real brother for whom Latin is obvious torture, and at a brother in spirit who is 'busy with two volumes' and 'did not look at all as if he were learning a lesson'.

This 'excited Maggie's curiosity'. The affinity between the two is one of imaginative and intellectual curiosity. Both Philip and Maggie are aware of limitless worlds lying outside everyday experience. Maggie can make Tom realise that Latin was a language spoken by living people, and Philip can bring to life for him the historical figures and events described in those texts with which he struggles. Philip paints Maggie twice, once from memory after her parting from him at the school at the age of twelve, and later from life among the Scotch firs — the first time, with her wild hair, as a 'gypsy', and the second as a hamadryad of the firs. He sees beneath accident into essence, and captures it from the flow of time. In the Red Deeps they discuss books read in common, applying their insights to their own lives, and reflect on art, music, and that general culture which provides an alternative to what Philip terms the 'dead level of provincial existence' (v, 3: 286). Philip provides some measure of relief to deprivations not only emotional, but also cultural and intellectual. But it is quite clear that he is a rarity in St Oggs. There is undoubtedly no simple way for Maggie to find the wholeness and fulfilment she seeks, but the novel strongly suggests that one stage in that quest would be to find a milieu in which enlightenment like Philip's is more widely dispersed. The indication never gets beyond such suggestiveness because, I believe, raised to full awareness, it would damagingly clash with one of the major values of the novel.

Maggie's glancing from Tom to Philip is a glancing from the known to the novel, from the familiar to the strange. She loves Tom; her curiosity is excited by Philip: the one is associated with home, the other with ventures outside it. In the background we may see, I think, analogous models from two literary modes, the pastoral and the quest romance. Pastoral differs from quest in the novel in being given strong and explicit authorial endorsement. The glance to Tom is loaded. It is loaded by the novel's well-known emphases, Wordsworthian in origin, on the importance of childhood surroundings and their associated objects. The familiar is given values not to be conventionally measured. As in Wordsworth, it is, first of all, inspirational. In the opening chapter place is given muse-like functions, calling up the settings and personages of the action through associational memory, which in turn takes on the role of Inspiration in traditional evocations, giving the author access to a Higher Power. As for her in her deepest life, so for the characters: the 'spots of time' in the novel are theirs as well as hers, similarly functioning to maintain not a novel but *their* story of *their* lives, a personal identity. This, we are assured in a well-known passage, develops from a familiarity with an 'outer world' which comes to seem 'only an extension of our own personality' which we accept as we do 'our own limbs'. Exotic 'ferns or splendid broad-petalled blossoms' indeed pall in comparison to 'furrowed and grassy fields', for these latter have been incorporated in the self, are constitutive of it (ii, 2: 135; i, 5: 38). Further, the familiar is seen as providing moral sustenance, acting as the soul of the moral being in keeping alive those ties of affection that constitute our elemental human duties. 'If the past is not to bind us', says Maggie to Stephen, as she prepares to leave him, 'where can duty lie?' (vi, 14: 417). And, finally, it has an almost institutional status, for its symbols and their significance endure though individual lives come and pass, as has the mill and its surroundings for five generations of Tullivers. When it is lost through Mr Tulliver's folly, and the family goods are auctioned, we sense no mere economic loss but rather spiritual dispossession; when Tom produces the money he has earned to pay the creditors as the first step towards its recovery, the family's feelings of pride and triumph speak of more than the simple restoration of honour. The novel, in short, makes a powerful investment in assumptions and values which interlock to constitute a system or virtually a creed. For Maggie to reject these for alternatives would risk making her role villainous or even heretical.

Yet such a set of assumptions and values has only conditional and not absolute validity. It is conditional geographically, as Aldous Huxley's 'Wordsworth in the Tropics' amusingly underlines, and it is conditional individually, as Maggie's history less amusingly demonstrates. Her persistent frustrations speak of a dissonance not experienced by other members of her family. George Eliot's general awareness of the relativity of credos and doctrines to the individual case, a cornerstone of her earliest thought, is curiously absent here. U. C. Knoepflmacher has pointed out that the novel's emphasis on the 'Wordsworthian myth of childhood' does not square with the reality of Maggie's relation with Tom.[7] This contradiction is consistent with the broader one between the Wordsworthian sanctification of place and the realities of her relations with family and community. Place is seen as both a source of strong positive values not to be abandoned, and as a source of spiritual constraint, intellectual atrophy and moral narrowness. It is as though the author, having had her faith in an immanent, purposeful universe destroyed through rational inquiry into Christianity, is reluctant to draw final conclusions from a similar investigation of doctrine which grants to the past a similar teleological authority. She stays uncomfortably in a double-consciousness, and Maggie, like a shuttlecock, is tossed back and forth by her conflicting allegiances to fact and to creed, positivism and faith.

Yet the glance to Philip works a quiet subversion. There has to be some awareness, conscious or unconscious, that perhaps another god has failed. There are minor signs. At one point, during one of Tom's recriminatory speeches, mention is made of events which must have taken place between volumes II and III: a quarrel between him and Maggie. He wished her to live with Aunt Pullet 'respectably amongst your relations'; she to take a teaching situation, which she did. For Tom this is evidence that she will not 'submit to be guided' (IV, 4: 342); for the reader that Maggie prefers independence even at the price of drudgery to staying at home as one of respectability's ornaments. More significantly, after Maggie's rejection of Stephen and return to St Ogg's, both the satiric exposure of community response and Dr Kenn's comments to Maggie that the present Christian community, having lost an original sense of fraternity, cannot appreciate the ethical value of her choice, raise to dangerous awareness the fact that with few exceptions (Mrs Glegg, Bob Jakin, Lucy) St Ogg's is not a source of moral well-being but rather the embodiment of a malign conventionality.

There are other ways, parodic, dramatic, and structural, in which the novelist underlines a central thesis of her novel. We may see an example even in the well-known passage in Book III, Chapter 9, which shows Mr Tulliver looking over the land he has lost, 'where all his memories centred, and where life seemed like a familiar smooth-handled tool' (III, 9: 233), and where he reminisces with Luke, his head miller, about his early life there. For Luke shares Mr Tulliver's sense of identification: 'I can't abide new places mysen: things is allays awk'ard—narrow-wheeled waggins, belike, and the stiles all another sort, an' oat-cake i' some places, tow'rt th' head o' the Floss, there. It's poor work, changing your country-side' (III, 9: 234). The author's scoring of our contempt for the familiar would hardly seem to endorse the alternative to Luke's attachment to it. He dislikes and suspects anything outside his blinkered experience, and views the eating of oat-cakes in regions only a few miles away in terms we might cautiously reserve for the rituals of some remote savage tribe. The passage echoes equally parochial assertions made in an earlier conversation with young Maggie, who tries to interest him in her books. To Maggie's assertion that 'we ought to know about our fellow creatures' such as the Dutchmen pictured in 'Pug's Tour of Europe' Luke replies with the xenophobic suspicion that Dutchmen are 'Not much o' fellow-creaturs', basing his view on the comprehensive research of his former master, who used to say 'If e'er I sow wheat wi'out brinin', I'm a Dutchman'. And to her offer of other enlarging reading he replies, 'An' they'r mostly lies, I think, what's printed i' the books'. Maggie tells him that he is like Tom, who is also not fond of reading (ɪ, 4: 27–8).

Similarly association and the attachment to objects it gives may be exaggeratedly valued. When Mrs Tulliver contemplates the loss of her china and linen at the auction to help pay the family debts, she is contemplating a separation as significant for her as the loss of the mill for her husband, and perhaps more so. (Mr Tulliver at least may continue to work on the land.) In both cases there is the loss of objects dear because well known, and invested with part of one's identity. In both cases there is strong authorial pathos. But with Mrs Tulliver there is also a hard, controlling irony. The chapter's title 'Mrs. Tulliver's Teraphim, or House-hold Gods', puts these objects in satiric perspective. China and linen seem unlikely candidates for deification, and the deities themselves, Hebrew household gods, graven images, belong to a more barbarous era than that of the enlightened narrator. The narrative content of the chapter emphasises another kind of limitation: Tom sympathises with his mother in her loss, and tacitly concurs with her complaints about Mr Tulliver's responsibility for it. Mr Tulliver is at this point levelled with a stroke, and Maggie finds the reproaches 'neutralised all her grief about table cloths and china', and speaks sharply to mother and brother about valuing things over people (ɪɪɪ, 2: 181). Objects may become fetishes, and human beings sacrificed to them. The same point seems to be more generally made in other satiric discussions of the Dodson attitude to possessions, so that we have a surprising implicit connection made between romantic associationism, in which objects endow life with meaning, and

Victorian acquisitiveness, in which, as in Veneering's dining room, they take life away. Mrs Glegg seems some way along in this decay of doctrine when she speaks with horror of the packman who 'murdered a young woman in a lone place, and *stole her thimble*, and threw her body into a ditch' (v, 2: 276. My italics).

We may also see the author's latent criticism of the doctrine in the two last books of the novel. In them there is a shift in emphasis, a structural distortion, which many readers have noticed. It is signalled by the rather abrupt entry of Stephen Guest into the work. Just as Maggie's positioning between Tom and Philip and what they represent was successor to the emblematic positioning between Dodson and Tulliver, so it is succeeded by a new positioning between Philip and Stephen. Philip, as we have seen, has some of the functions of Tom in Maggie's mind: he exists there in continuity from childhood as an enlightened alternative brother. Stephen has similar qualities of enlightenment, or what Maggie takes for such: he shares with her sophistication in wit and the love of music, but his novelty precludes any association with the childhood pastoral. He is more fully 'outside'. So the feelings he arouses are not those of ideal sympathy and domestic affection, but those of sexual passion, with its risky ventures into the unknown. The shift in emphasis which comes from attending to Maggie's relation to him results in a narrowing and intensifying of the focus of the novel. We move from a work of frequent panoramic scope, which presented the natural world of the countryside near the river and the Red Deeps, the family world around the mill, and the social world of St Ogg's and the surrounding districts, to the Deanes' drawing room and occasionally a section of St Ogg's 'best society'. The pastoral theme is not absent, but it is certainly diminished: what would seem to be its climax, the recovery of the mill from Wakem, occurs in this section, but it is not treated with the intensity due to a culmination. The intensity (and, I submit, the novelist's imaginative engagement) resides elsewhere.

We now hear more about the inner life than ever before, and we tend to hear about it in a different way. No section of the novel is without those characteristic elements we call 'analytic' —that combination of behavioural demonstration, inner presentation, and authorial explanation which shows the mind at work on the margins of self-knowledge, sometimes clearing a way towards it, and sometimes moving itself slowly and cunningly

away. But the inner elements of that procedure are stronger here
because we examine, for the first sustained time in the work, two
minds in mutuality of attraction, its disavowal, and unconscious
assertion.

> If Stephen came in when Lucy was out of the room — if Lucy
> left them together, they never spoke to each other: Stephen,
> perhaps, seemed to be examining books or music, and Maggie
> bent her head assiduously over her work. Each was oppressively
> conscious of the other's presence, even to the finger-ends. Yet
> each looked and longed for the same thing to happen the next
> day. Neither of them had begun to reflect on the matter, or
> silently to ask, 'To what does all this tend?' (vi, 6: 352).[8]

It is passages like this which lie behind Joan Bennett's observation
that we are here moving towards the concerns of the later works,
and that indeed in many ways we are looking at another
embryonic, more 'modern' novel.[9] Much has been said about
their sexual component, and it is indeed by Victorian standards
very candidly and by any standards very insightfully presented.
But this very un-Victorian treatment of courtship also represents
a boldness and venturesomeness on the part of the author, is at
one with her constant realistic quest to test conventional perception, whether social or literary, and expose its distortions. Her
daring has its correspondences with that of her characters, not
only in their trip down the river to Mudport, but also in Maggie's
return home in umarried state, reaction to which not only reveals
the self-righteousness of St Ogg's but also finally challenges the
very pastoral conventions on which the novel is based.

   When Philip looks at Maggie he thinks of her as a princess
turned into an animal. *The Thousand and One Nights* were
widely available to Victorian readers in Edward Lane's bowd-
lerised but well-annotated translation of 1839–41, and it is probably to this translation that George Eliot makes allusion in
letters of 1852, 1854 and 1859 (*Letters* ii: 65, 164; viii: 239).
Transformations through magical charms are common in the
tales, and it is not difficult to find some about humans changed
into animals. Such transformations trap them in degraded forms
in communities which do not recognise their true nature. Philip
recognises the essential nature of Maggie which is constantly
transformed by community incantation. Tom teases her and

seeks to make her 'obey', treats her like a pet, really. For others in family and community she is a 'small mistake of nature' (not one of her rarer creations), a 'gypsy' (not a member of humanity, with a dark skin), oddly 'quick' for a girl (instead of an intelligent being), or a traitor to a family curse (not someone who values conciliation over tribal war) [*passim*]. The town's response to her return echoes these earlier reifications. For its ladies (the 'world's wife') the unsavoury prophecies long announced by Miss Tulliver's very physique have come to pass; for the gentlemen there is occasion for jokes and smiles, and as for Tom, he renounces proprietorship: 'You don't belong to me' (vii, 2: 429; 2–4 *passim*; 1: 423). The point would seem to be made (and is made explicitly by Dr Kenn), to go where spells will no longer be cast, but, as all know, it is ultimately ignored.

The Mill on the Floss emphasises the psychological and ethical side of Worsworthian doctrine: it deals with the assumption that Nature (which, as in Wordsworth, includes community) will never betray the heart that loves her. But positivist awareness that in *Adam Bede* placed Stonyshire next to Loamshire to remind us that Nature is not necessarily benign creates in the novel a community equally indifferent to the purpose of Wordsworth's Nature. The novel is a record of its persistent betrayal of the loving heart, which by an act of faith seeks evidence of that purpose and fails to find it. The novelist shares Maggie's faith, and no more than her will she finally abandon it. She reaffirms it strongly at the novel's end where Nature answers Maggie's prayer with the flood that reunites brother and sister and, incidentally, punishes the apostates of St Ogg's. But the author will never again put the doctrine to such a painful test. Pastoral in the subsequent fiction is reserved for truly rustic characters capable of harmony with the community, like Silas Marner, or reduced to minor significance, as in the record of the ride of Fred and Rosamond Vincy at the opening of Chapter 12 of *Middlemarch*. It is never again to be 'home' for a consciousness which transcends it.

NOTES

1   John Blackwood to George Eliot, 7 March 1860, *The George Eliot Letters*, 9 vols (New Haven: Yale University Press, 1954–78), iii, 272.
2   *The Mill on the Floss*, introd. Gordon S. Haight, Riverside edn. (Boston: Houghton Mifflin, 1961), ii, 5: 158. All citations are to this edition.

3 In *A Century of George Eliot Criticism*, ed. Gordon S. Haight (London: Methuen, 1966), pp. 349–60.

4 In *Essays of George Eliot*, ed. Thomas Pinney (London: Routledge, 1963), pp. 261–5.

5 Barbara Hardy, 'The Mill on the Floss,' in *Critical Essays on George Eliot*, ed. Barbara Hardy (London: Routledge, 1970), pp. 42–58. See especially pp. 53–56.

6 For discussion of the source and significance of this myth see Joseph Wiesenfarth, 'Legend in *The Mill on the Floss*', *Texas Studies in Literature and Language*, 18 (Spring 1976), 20–41; rpt. and rvd in *George Eliot's Mythmaking* (Heidelberg: Carl Winter-Universitätsverlag, 1977), pp. 96–123.

7 In *George Eliot's Early Novels* (Berkeley: University of California Press, 1968), p. 217.

8 The chapter from which this is taken is entitled 'Illustrating the Laws of Attraction'. Despite her unfavourable review of Stendhal's 'Ernestine, ou la Naissance de l'Amour' in the *Westminster Review*, 65 (April 1856), 642–3) George Eliot may have retained an impression of its reduction of love to a set of psychological laws.

9 Joan Bennett, *George Eliot* (Cambridge University Press, 1948), p. 130.

12   The Unity of *Felix Holt*

FLORENCE SANDLER

The commentators on *Felix Holt, the Radical* have fallen for the most part into two groups, each more or less dissatisfied.[1] There are those who, taking their cue from the title, expect the book to have a radical hero with effective political as well as personal quality, and the action to entail a modern political analysis of the structure of personality and society. Such readers are likely to conclude that Felix is an ineffective radical and ineffective hero, and that the action falls apart from that defective centre.

Then there are those (the more self-consciously literary critics) who take their cue ultimately from F. R. Leavis. He vindicated the part of the book that comprised the 'profoundly moving tragedy' of Mrs Transome, and proceeded to damn the rest with faint praise. The elaboration of the main plot was perversely, if not desiccatingly, misdirected. The presentation of Felix himself (unbelievably 'noble and courageous in act as in ideal', 'wholly endorsed by his creator') supported the complaint against Eliot's intellectualism. Rufus Lyon, who occupied so much of the book, was 'incredible and a bore', and 'Esther, the beautiful and elegant young lady passing as his daughter', was 'interesting only in relation to other feminine studies of the author's and to her treatment in general of feminine charm'![2] Apparently, that meant being hardly interesting at all. The lopsided view of the book inherited from Leavis was reinforced by Fred Thomson's judgement that the Transome tragedy, being the original material of the book, remained the intrinsic part, while the political theme, added later, seemed 'adventitious'.[3] More recently, we have been trying to put the pieces of the novel together, and my purpose in the present essay is to argue for its architectonic unity. The appreciation of this unity rests on three interrelated considerations: the centrality of Esther, and the significance of her final decision; the role of Rufus Lyon; and the nature of the radicalism of Felix Holt. Each of these will be considered in turn.

My contention at the outset is that it is Esther whose story gives the book a beginning, a middle and an end. In this symmetrical plot two sons, Harold Transome and Felix Holt, have returned home to North Loamshire to take charge of the fortunes of their families, both disappointing the expectations that their mothers have set on the event. But a daughter, Esther, has also returned home to North Loamshire. Both Harold and Felix become radical candidates for the parliamentary seat; both become suitors of Esther Lyon. Her marriage-choice (so George Eliot arranges things) will eventually depend on her recognition of the ethical quality of the two, and that quality will have become apparent in their attitude toward the electorate as well as in their attitude to Esther herself. Esther is in fact confronted not only with a choice of suitors but a choice of parents; she must choose to belong to the community of Harold and his mother on the one hand, or Felix and Rufus Lyon on the other.

We follow the progressive clarification of Esther's vision from comparative ignorance until she sees clearly the mediocrity of Harold and the self-destructiveness of his mother contrasted with the heroism to be found both in her father and Felix. She has her own moment of heroism at last, when she stands up to testify for Felix at his trial.[4]

The complaint of ineffectiveness against Felix, the 'titular hero' of the book, arises from a misunderstanding. There is a class of titles that derive not from the protagonist but from the person, or sometimes the entity, that has most effect upon the protagonist, presenting an attraction, an enigma or challenge that prompts him or her to self-exploration. Thus Coleridge's 'Christabel', Brontë's *The Professor*, Melville's 'Bartleby the Scrivener', and Eliot's *Daniel Deronda*. In this class *Felix Holt* also belongs. As a character, Felix can no longer be written off as merely static since Eliot gives development to both his personality and philosophical position. Nevertheless, the presentation is unsatisfactory, for with the first interior monologue after he has met Esther we are promised access to his subjectivity, but through the book are often fobbed off with an exterior view, or given an account of his motives that is uncritical and therefore incredible. But Felix's frequent escape from the ironic scrutiny that controls other characters is not so serious a problem when he is not in fact the main protagonist.

As Felix tells Esther at one point, his own story was mostly over before he met her, but from that he has gained a certain vision which he hopes she too may come to share. Felix's problem now is to put together the two disparate parts of his life, so that his attraction to Esther no longer threatens his sense of mission. In the design of the book, where he is pitted against Harold, both men start off with their 'illusions' and a 'too-confident self-reliance', but Felix's illusions are based on an altruistic object, and Harold's on an egoistic one. In private life, as in politics, Harold's style is 'the utmost enjoyment of his own advantages'. Both have their illusions shattered: Felix cannot control the riots, and Harold cannot control his own political agent and the facts of his birth. The experience of his own limitations leads Felix to a less ambitious form of service, and Harold to something like despair. ('For the first time the iron had entered into his soul.')

The same difference obtains between the two older people in each group, Rufus Lyon and Mrs Transome, who have absorbed their disappointment and taken account of their limitations before the present story begins. They are two contrasting kinds of sinners: she the self-absorbed one, for whom 'the great story of this world' was reduced 'to the little tale of her own existence', and who had no analysis of things that went beyond blood and family; he the one whom the 'danger of absorption within the narrow bounds of self urged . . . the more towards action which had a wider bearing, and might tell on the welfare of England at large'.

In the symmetry of the plot, both Rufus and Mrs Transome are confronted with the problem of whether to tell a beloved child the secret of the child's paternity. In each case, the parent has a tenuous hold on the child's affections and is afraid that telling the secret will mean losing that affection altogether. Rufus makes a clean breast of his 'fall' and the circumstances of Esther's adoption and, to his surprise, wins more interest and affection from Esther than he has ever known. She is impressed by how much he must have loved her mother, and excited by her sudden 'illumination' that that must be 'the very best life . . . where one bears and does everything because of some great and strong feeling — so that this and that in one's circumstances don't signify'.

Mrs Transome's refusal to tell Harold her secret is based on a double shame: not only did she fall once, but she hates the man who used her and turned her love into a good bargain, and she hates herself for having been used. Here too the son's discovery of his paternity is the occasion when he first looks at his mother for what she is in herself, but in pity, and on the basis of a common misery. Esther, who learned something of spiritual heroism from Rufus Lyon's confession, will learn at the end, from Mrs Transome's plea for comfort, the effect of spiritual desolation.

That last embrace between Esther and Mrs Transome is the climax of the movement which has brought them to see each other as, in a sense, mother and daughter. Esther had been presented at first as an elegant young woman (very much like the young Arabella Transome in her bearing and self-image), yet deprived because of never having known the mother whom she felt she could have loved better than her father. By the end, Esther has found her 'mother' in Mrs Transome and can treat her as a daughter would; but she has also transcended her need of this mother. When she folds Mrs Transome in her arms and leads her to bed, it is as if she, Esther, were the mother and Mrs Transome the child. Then Esther leaves Transome Court and returns to Rufus Lyon, the 'father' with whom she has discovered a deeper affinity.

I confess that I enjoy Rufus Lyon immensely. I enjoy even his casuistry, his long-windedness, his seventeenth-century idiom, and Eliot's loving reproduction and gentle satire of those long biblical conceits. The author presumably thought that Rufus's credit with the reader would sustain parody in Mrs Holt, for just as that formidable woman caricatures Mrs Transome in posing as the mother pushed aside by the son she dotes on, she caricatures Rufus and presents the Dissenting style at its worst with her interminable talk and her obsession with her own righteousness. But Rufus is not convinced of his own righteousness, let alone anxious to parade it, and there is always point in what he says. One comes to know his idiosyncrasy in language and thought so well as to share his vision of the world. Rufus is the comic counterweight of the tragic Mrs Transome in all senses of the word comic: he is often ludicrous; at the same time, he is the character whose values make for community and life, whereas hers make for isolation and death-in-life; and, in setting an example for Esther by his espousal of Felix's cause, he is instrumental in resolving the plot satisfactorily.

Granted that Rufus is restricted to the idiom of Milton and the seventeenth-century Dissenters, his strength lies in the fact that he has never lost the high vision of that time. Recognising a fellow-spirit in Felix, far more than anyone in his congregation, he

challenges him to assume that heritage, not for the sake of glori-
fying the past but for shaping the future:

> 'You will not deny that you glory in the name of Radical, or
> Root-and-branch man, as they said in the great times when
> Nonconformity was in its giant youth.'
> 'A Radical—yes; but I want to go to some roots a good deal
> lower down than the franchise.'
> 'Truly there is a work within which cannot be dispensed
> with; but it is our preliminary work to free men from the stifled
> life of political nullity, and bring them into what Milton calls
> "the liberal air," wherein alone can be wrought the final
> triumphs of the Spirit' (27: 368–9).

It perfectly characterises Rufus Lyon that, given the oppor-
tunity to request a favour from the Debarrys, he should ask for a
debate on, 'first, the constitution of the true church; and se-
condly, the bearing thereupon of the English Reformation'. This
is not at all the issue in the year of the national debate on the
Reform Bill; and yet, in his own sectarian terms, Rufus is asking
for consideration of the nature of human community and the
bearing thereupon of a particular history, especially in this case
the experience of the Reformation. On the one hand, the Reformation had given rise to the present ecclesiastical alignments and
much of the arrangement of class, property and power, and on
the other hand it had provided the precedent for the present Reform—all of which is very much the issue.

It is equally characteristic of the Church of England vicar, who
enjoys the advantages of the political and social arrangements,
that the last thing he wants to do is to participate in such a
debate, where he is not at all sure of winning and where losing
will bring the Church's tenure of advantages into question. The
Reverend Augustus Debarry first of all tries demurrer, complaining that Lyon has put 'non-natural strained sense on a
promise', and, when that will not do, offers up his curate as a
lamb to the slaughter, reassuring the young man that this is one
of the great opportunities of his career. When the poor curate in
turn suffers a failure of nerve and slips out of town, the vicar's
dignity is unperturbed: he is 'sorry for poor Sherlock who wanted
confidence', but convinced that 'for his own part he had taken the
course which under the circumstances was the least compro-

mising to the church'. Where intellectual substance is lacking, one needs a consummate gift for saving appearances; the opponent, who does have something to say and is not afraid to say it, is left embarrassed by the fact that there is only vacuum to say it to.

The outcome of the debate, or the lack of it, is prepared for by the original description of the lovely old rectory, with its bow window, deep-turfed lawn, and Virginia creeper, lying 'close to the church of which it was the fitting companion', with the author's mischievous comment that it was 'one of those rectories which are among the bulwarks of our venerable institutions — which arrest disintegrating doubt, serve as a double embankment against Popery and Dissent, and rally feminine instinct and affection to reinforce the decisions of masculine thought'. Fortunately, the bulwark itself is so impressive in appearance that when 'the decisions of masculine thought' are dispensed with altogether, no one seems to notice the difference.

Contrary to those who see the abandonment of the debate as one of the 'comic possibilities which are never in fact realized',[5] I find it an excellent comic effect as it stands. Moreover, it prepares for the final episode of the book, since Rufus's appearance to give testimony for Dissent in the debate is a prelude to his appearance to give testimony at Felix's trial. He is a faithful friend and pastor to the young man over the objections of his congregation, which sees no Christian principle involved because Felix is not one of them (so much for the Good Samaritan!), and blames Felix because it feels implicated in the riot which is bound to be discussed at the trial.

Rufus's heart is 'bruised' for his defence of Felix, but this is appropriate treatment from his sect for one who has transcended sectarianism, that egoism in the collective. Rufus lives heroically, not only by the criteria of the great Dissenters by which he measures himself, but also according to the Comtean criteria of George Eliot's world. When asked at the trial whether Felix is one of his congregation, his answer indicates that he has recognised the spiritual continuity that transcends particular historical traditions, even if, to Eliot's mind, he catches the continuity by the wrong end and thinks of Felix's modern, secular virtue as issuing into the historical church, instead of the other way round.

And so to the issue of Felix's radicalism. When Felix in the 1830s can discount the Chartist platform and declare that he is not interested in whether the Radical candidate gets elected, he is not the sort of person that a member of the Labour Party would want to count among the political ancestors. Felix's politics (and George Eliot's) suffer, it has been asserted, from the 'tendency to value the purely moral above the merely social', and to believe that 'far-flung corporate matters can be solved by a "change of heart," by starting from individual selves, or by setting up an abstraction the pursuit of which is supposed to be mankind's way of getting forward'.[6]

To defend Felix's radicalism in these circumstances is to become an exponent of George Eliot's political position, at least to the extent that this is necessary in describing the artistic unity of the novel. Without making the claim that George Eliot is a sophisticated political theorist or analyst of political structures, the literary critic can still give her credit for the coherent political viewpoint represented in Felix Holt as a character and in the action of the novel. Felix's iconoclastic style is epitomised in his treatment of the family patent medicines, something that his mother will never give over lamenting. 'Are the pills good for people?' was the only question that Felix asked; and since they were not, he threw them out, regardless of revenue, family piety, or the 'dread of appearing ridiculous' in admitting the fraud. Thereafter, through the novel, we see various characters put to the test in a situation comparable to that of Felix with the pills. In Harold's case, it is a matter of deciding whether electioneering by way of treating the miners is 'good for people'. Does it do what it purports to do? If not, it is fradulent. By the time that Harold gives evidence at the trial, he is in a position to see the element of fraud in his own campaign as a Reform candidate, dedicated to 'rooting out abuses'. In the hands of the unreformed Jermyn and Johnson, it has led directly to the brutalisation of the electorate and to mob violence.

Harold's conclusion is presumably that, if one wants to be practical and get oneself into a position of more power, one must make some moral compromises, even as a Radical. Felix, who had put the picture together earlier and warned Harold about the likely consequences of the treating, had drawn the opposite conclusion: if one wants to maintain moral integrity, one had better not jockey for a position of power, even as a Radical leader. The two conclusions seem to be equally logical; and it is a matter of character as to whether it will seem more important to hold on to power or to moral integrity.

Felix's decision in favour of moral integrity makes him, as has been said, not a radical at all in the political sense. He is, as he says at one point, more 'radical' than that. What he has come up with is a radical critique of the political and economic process. He will stay out of the push and scramble, the buying and selling of people, in both spheres. Rather than a failed Francis Place, Felix might be regarded as a nineteenth-century version of the Lollard Piers Plowman (also an honest working man), or of those Egyptian hermits in late Antiquity so-called because they threw in their lot with the poor of the countryside as a social and moral protest. Felix himself, defining his radicalism as altogether secular, recognises nevertheless that the tradition includes Saint Theresa and Elizabeth Fry, and sends Esther a message from prison about espousing poverty as if he were a Franciscan. Trying to understand Esther's view of Felix, Harold suggests that Felix is 'quite an apostolic sort of fellow'.

The 'Gothic' head of Felix brings another train of associations, and implies the affinity between Felix and Rufus Lyon. This is not *Castle of Otranto* Gothic, but the 'Gothic' of Milton and his contemporaries, invoking an original Germanic stock, strong, freedom loving and republican, a norm against which to judge the tyranny and servility of the present age, and by which to purge the Constitution of the abuses inherited from the invader William and his feudal lords. Felix asserts the 'Gothic liberties' and rights that Milton defended — liberties retrieved, so Whig orthodoxy insisted, in the Settlement of 1688, but older than that Settlement and capable of being invoked against it.[7] Felix's perspective on privilege in the state is matched by Rufus's opinion of the privileged choir in the congregation:

> [Their] special office it is to lead the singing, not because they are more disposed to the devout uplifting of praise, but because they are endowed with better vocal organs, and have attained more of the musician's art. For all office, unless it be accompanied by peculiar grace, becomes, as it were, a diseased organ, seeking to make itself too much of a centre. Singers, specially so called, are, it must be confessed, an anomaly among us who seek to reduce the Church to its primitive simplicity, and to cast away all that may obstruct the direct communion of spirit with spirit (13: 240).

Rufus has no less perspicacity than Felix into fallen man and his institutions, but he has more tolerance of the situation, having understood how far he himself is implicated in the fall.

It is not that Felix disapproves of Reform at Duffield. He says, 'Hear, Hear', emphatically to the proposition that 'the greatest question in the world is, how to give every man a man's share in what goes on in life'. He disagrees, however, that the Reform platform (universal suffrage, annual parliaments, and so on) will achieve that without a reformation of the national character, and insists that voting for Transome is no means to reform. If the political process and political representative are corrupt, no reform worth the name will have been achieved. Accordingly, Felix's own speech at Duffield fixes for its most telling point on the character of Harold's political agents.

Felix's point is borne out in the action of the book not only when the mob riots, but when Harold himself discovers that the men whom he has employed as his agents are as capable of using him as he them, and that the candidacy which he had undertaken in order to gain more power has put him in the power of the political professionals. Jermyn and Johnson work by manipulation and blackmail, against the other candidates, against each other, against their employer if necessary — and they find the means to blackmail Harold by investigating his family's claim to Transome Court. Harold can outplay men like this only at the risk of losing his own integrity. In the last confrontation, when Harold is rendered powerless by Jermyn's last weapon, the assertion of his paternity, the horror for Harold consists in the realisation of how much like his father he has become.

The legal manoeuvrings in the nineteenth century reveal an earlier set of legal manoeuvrings in the eighteenth and so back, presumably, to infinity. As long as land, property, and power have been maintained, it has been by means of such manipulation — which is Felix's point about the pushing and scrambling. The critic who complains that 'the law, which dominate[s] the plot, is never itself given any serious moral or historical consideration', such as Dickens gave to the law in a similar situation in *Bleak House*,[8] has failed to take account of the thematic ironies involved.

How far Felix is 'ineffectual' is a question that the book constantly reconsiders by new criteria and perspectives. The subject is taken up when Felix is awaiting trial for manslaughter in the course of the riot he had failed to control. Esther's mention of the

prospect of failure is, he admits, a 'dreadfully inspired' temptation, but he has now seen through that word failure. One must
simply do what one believes in and refuse to accept effect as the cri-
terion of value: 'I'd rather have the minimum of effect, if it's of the
sort I care for, than the maximum of effect I don't care for' — a remark we recognise as a description of the differences between
Felix's 'ineffectualness' and Harold's. All the same, Felix has
decided to limit the possibilities of failure. He doesn't intend to be
illustrious and shape a new era, but only to do small things, and
those by way of proving a point of the utmost importance for the
working classes: namely, that 'there's some dignity and happiness
for a man other than changing his station'.

The riot in Treby Magna has changed his mind about the most
appropriate expression of his radical vision. Partly, he has been
led to the scene of the riot by the desire to distract himself from
the thought of Esther. The recognition of his motive and the comparative failure of his intervention in the riot point him now
towards a quieter, more domestic version of radical activity and
an acknowledgement of his love for Esther. He has accepted what
might be called the Reformation version of the Franciscan style,
where the counterculture begins not with the celibate lay friar but
with the community of husband and wife. Felix's purging of
motives, his undertaking of a full human life, even if obscure,
need not be seen as an abdication from politics. In the long run,
judging from the history of those who have been invoked, (Saint
Francis, John the Baptist, and the original 'apostolic sort of
fellows'), such a life might prove to be the most powerful threat to
the Jermyns and Johnsons and the politics of corruption. Milton
in *Paradise Regained* and Bunyan in the episode of Vanity Fair in
The Pilgrim's Progress had made this point; Eliot wants to leave it
open as least as a possibility that the meek may inherit the earth.

Having described Felix's radicalism, one comes to the vexed
question of whether its implications are carried through in
Esther's decision, or whether that decision shows some unrelated
'personal preference' on Esther's part; whether, in short, the resolution is any resolution at all, and the novel can be said to
continue to the end according to a unifying design. Felix's political judgement is more radical than most, because it goes beyond
political labels to test the character of people and institutions,
and Esther's judgement is similarly 'radical' in the deliberation of
her marriage choice. The defect that Felix had observed in

Harold's political campaign, Esther observes in Harold's dealings in his own family, even with his mother. The handsome, agreeable Harold invariably pursues his own objectives, using and discarding people like commodities. His most sincere attempt to commend his own sensibility constitutes the worst incrimination, when he assures Esther of the value he sets upon her, far beyond that other woman, Harry's mother, who 'had been a slave—was bought, in fact'. Shades of the Giaour! Esther's insight is that it is Harold, the aristocrat, who is mercenary and 'vulgar', and Felix, the working man, who is 'noble'. The words, with all their class connotation, are intended, I think, to be taken seriously. Esther's realisation of the moral corruption that obtains in Transome Court carries the implication that the class structure somehow subverts the true order of society. As the seventeenth-century radicals said, the world has been 'turned upside down'.

She has arrived at this perception also in aesthetic terms. In court, she has noted the 'striking contrast' between Harold and Felix: Harold 'like a handsome portrait by Sir Thomas Lawrence'; Felix like a sculpture from 'the later Roman period, when the plastic impulse was stirred by the grandeur of barbaric forms'. Her original notion of beauty had been satisfied by the elegant turn of her ankle, by her laces, gloves, and flattering blues, all of which would have qualified her to be the figure complementary to Harold in a Lawrence portrait. Now she has come to appreciate in Felix not merely the beautiful but the sublime. The 'barbaric grandeur' of Felix, his 'massive frame' and 'Gothic head', suggest that style ('sublime', 'Gothic', 'Michaelangelesque') which Blake had pitted against the Academy's beautiful and effete; and, as with Blake, the contrast has political reference. The Academy style flatters (and is supported by) the aristocracy that wields political power secured in the Settlement of 1688; the 'sublime', however, invokes the heroic, even godlike, man (Eliot, like Blake, uses the Miltonic phrase 'Human Face Divine'), beyond class distinction and potentially subversive of it.

This new 'vision of hers, which makes things hitherto great look mean', had been confirmed by Felix in prison. When he talked of the need to do what one believes in, regardless of the 'effect' on the world, and declared that it would jar his nature to hold on to certain fine things 'while the world is what it is', his words 'at last seemed strangely to fit her own experience'. What follows from this clarification of judgement is the courage to act upon it, first when she stands up to testify for Felix in court, and then when she decides that, whether or not Felix loves her, she will of her own accord leave Transome Court with its mercenariness, luxury, and misery, forget any claim upon the Bycliffe Transome estate, and go back to a poorer but more livable life with her father in Malthouse Yard.

Even V. S. Pritchett underestimates the self-realisation to which Eliot leads Esther Lyon, mistaking it for a kind of utilitarianism. Impressed by the Victorian analogy between moral and economic improvement, he finds Esther in her urge to 'self-improvement' to be 'impelled by the competitive reforming ethic of an expanding society'; for 'George Eliot writes at a time when Fortune has been torn down, when the earned increment of industry . . . has taken Fortune's place; and when character is tested not by hazard but, like the funds, by a measurable tendency to rise and fall'.[9] What Pritchett overlooks is that Eliot deplores the tendency for the economy of money and character to coincide, and she is among the foremost critics of that commercialised version of the doctrine of Providence that expected prosperity in this world to be a sign of election. When Pritchett proceeds to generalise from Esther Lyon's case that 'in all the mid-Victorian novels the characters are either going up in the world, in which case they are good; or they are going down in the world in which case they are bad', he overlooks the fact that in the present novel Eliot's point was exactly the opposite; for, after much of the book has been given to the exposure of just what kind of character it takes for Jermyn and Johnson to 'go up' in the world, Esther does right to turn down that consummate 'man of the world', Harold Transome, and choose instead Felix Holt, who has decided not to 'go up' in the world on any terms but to remain a working man all his life.

Equally mistaken is the complaint that the resolution of the novel does not hold because 'at the trial, as throughout almost all the latter part of the novel, the actual implications of Felix's Radicalism are lost sight of', and that it is merely 'to his "nobility" that Esther testifies at his trial, not his principles: what she gives him is a high-grade character-reference'.[10] Partly, this comment understimates the significance of Esther's giving Felix a 'high-grade character-reference', when most enterprises in the novel, personal and political, are shown to have foundered precisely on defect of character; partly, it fails to appreciate the nature of

Felix's radical vision; and partly, it has not taken into account how far Esther, through her own experience, comes to share that vision.

One might test the claim for structural unity in the novel in another fashion, by picking up Fred Thomson's suggestion of reading it as a tragedy in Aeschylean style. In the *Agamemnon* and the Transome part of *Felix Holt* Thomson saw a similar 'controlling theme of "hereditary, entailed Nemesis" that collides with "the peculiar individual lot"', Mrs Transome and Harold being each one the victim but also the perpetuator of Nemesis. But since most of the novel could not be accounted for in terms of the *Agamemnon*, Thomson concluded that it was largely a failure.[11] In the *Oresteia*, however, Eliot had a model not only for the impact of Nemesis in the *Agamemnon* and *The Libation Bearers*, but also for the transcendence of Nemesis in *The Eumenides*, when Athena vindicates Orestes and upholds the superiority of the new order of Apollo over the old order represented by the Furies and Clytemnestra's ghost.

Mrs Transome will do very well for Clytemnestra, having taken the mediocre Jermyn (for Aegisthus) as her lover and the administator of the estate, and killed her husband, at least in spirit. When her son, returning after many years of absence, treats her with a deadly indifference, she comes to wish that he had never been born. Like Clytemnestra's ghost, she lives in gloom, pounces on Jermyn like a Fury, and stalks the house at night seeking comfort.

Equally, Esther will do very well as Athena, her testimony for Felix in court providing the climax of the drama, as does Athena's judgement for Orestes. Like the goddess deciding between the two orders represented by Clytemnestra's Furies and Apollo, Esther chooses over the corruption of the Transomes the 'Apollonian' principle represented by Felix with his vision of a better humanity. Like Athena she qualifies to be the judge because she herself participates in both orders, being like Mrs Transome a woman, yet intellectually her father's child. Before she leaves Transome Court, however, she embraces Mrs Transome, lays her down to rest, and gives her the reconciliation with her son for which she longs—as Athena, having judged against the Furies, gives them rest and reverence within the new city.

In the *Oresteia*, the young women of the first two parts, Cassandra and Elektra, are the victims of Nemesis; they are succeeded in the third part by the goddess whose apotheosis means that the curse can be dispelled — or, to be more precise, can be contained and made innocuous within a wider experience. In the novel, Esther too is a potential victim, her initial values and self-image being very much like those of the young Mrs Transome. But it is the other possibility that triumphs when Esther finds the courage to be a witness for Felix at his trial, and thereafter the temptations offered by Harold and Transome Court are innocuous. Esther too has her apotheosis (when she stands up to give testimony, it is 'as if a vibration, quick as light, had gone through the court'), but, being no goddess, she has come by her apotheosis and discernment only by experience and self-criticism.

This is not to imply that the *Oresteia* is the exclusive model for Eliot's novel, though the comparison points to the kind of structural unity that Eliot achieves in *Felix Holt*. A comparison with *Paradise Lost* would also hold, and one wonders why Thomson failed to consider the constructive influence of Shakespeare, whom Eliot was also reading in this period. Ultimately the unity of the novel is of the Shakespearean kind, where thematic and imagistic continuities run between plot and subplot, between tragic characters and comic ones, and where scenes of high drama among the principal characters may be offset by scenes in the tap room where lowly folk can comment on the issues in their own style.

In claiming a structural unity for *Felix Holt*, I am not assuming that the book is flawless. Most readers are dissatisfied with the ending and particularly with the cloying tone of those final passages where, in the courtroom, an ardour of spirit burns 'in the bosom of sweet Esther Lyon'; where Esther and Felix hold hands and 'look straight into each other's eyes, as angels do when they tell some truth'; or when she answers him 'with a laugh as sweet as the morning thrush'. But an appreciation of the architectonic unity of the book suggests a different reason for this failure of tone. It is not that the book has fallen apart by this time and that Eliot has recourse to romantic stuffing. The problem is the opposite one. Plot and theme have come together all too well.

The heroine, once a denizen of Vanity Fair, has since become a pilgrim of the spirit, proceeding by the 'illuminations' that she gains from her father's life and Felix's, wrestling with the temptations of Transome Court and overcoming them to the point where she provides an illumination of her own in her appearance in

court, and will accept nothing less in her life or her husband than
a 'high enthusiasm'. The problem is that the heroine now sees as
the author sees — and the controlling irony is withdrawn. Eliot is
as uncritical of Esther's final situation as is Esther herself. She has
told us that Esther is one of those women 'whose fulness of perfection must be in marriage', and that her rightful choice is the man
who is nobler than herself. Esther, doing better than Rufus Lyon
or Arabella Transome, selects the marriage partner in whom her
love and judgement concur. ('In this, at least, her woman's lot
was perfect: that the man she loved was her hero; that her woman's passion and her reverence for rarest goodness rushed together in an undivided current.') The marriage-choice which
gives unity to Esther's life also gives unity to the novel. But this is a
phenomenon disconcerting to the reader who does not want a
novel to be built like a morality play and prefers the ending that is
problematic.

All one can say here is that Eliot is her own best critic. From
Felix Holt she proceeded to *Middlemarch*, taking up the story of
Dorothea Brooke, who believes that her spiritual fulfilment is to
be found in giving herself in marriage to someone nobler than
herself. Esther's 'truth' has become Dorothea's illusion. That marvellous irony of George Eliot's will not be stunned by any illumination for long.

NOTES

1   I am grateful to the National Endowment for the Humanities for the Fel-
    lowship that allowed me to write this paper. Quotations are taken from
    Felix Holt, ed. Peter Coveney (Harmondsworth: Penguin Books, 1972).
2   F. R. Leavis, *The Great Tradition* (London: Chatto & Windus, 1948),
    50–61.
3   Fred C. Thomson, 'The Genesis of *Felix Holt*', *PMLA*, 74 (1959), 576–84.
4   Arnold Kettle sees the initial symmetry of action between 'the Transome
    area' and 'the Lyon–Holt area', but considers that from about the twelfth
    chapter the novel deteriorates because it loses sight of the issue of Felix's
    radicalism. He assumes that Felix is the protagonist. (Arnold Kettle, 'Felix
    Holt, the Radical', *Critical Essays on George Eliot*, ed. Barbara Hardy
    [New York: Barnes & Noble; London: Routledge & Kegan Paul, 1970],
    pp. 99–115.) David Carroll, who carries through to the end of the novel the
    parallels between Harold and Felix and sees Esther placed in the position of
    choosing between them, is still so far bound to the conventional reading
    that he finds Esther's final choice of Felix an 'anti-climax' and considers
    that in the last third of the novel she has 'usurped' the 'central position' of

the 'titular hero' and thrown the novel off balance! (David R. Carroll, *'Felix Holt*: Society as Protagonist', *Nineteenth-Century Fiction*, 17 (1962), 237–52, rep. in *George Eliot: A Collection of Critical Essays*, ed. George R. Creeger [Englewood Cliffs, N.J.: Prentice-Hall, 1970], pp. 124–40.)

Writing more recently, Laura Emory asserts the centrality of Esther's role throughout the novel and the significance of her choice between Rufus Lyon and Mrs Transome as a parent, but Emory's doggedly Freudian interpretation causes her to underestimate, in particular, the constructive role of Rufus Lyon. (Laura Comer Emory, *George Eliot's Creative Conflict: The Other Side of Silence* [Berkeley, Los Angeles, London: University of California Press, 1976], 107 ff.)

A balanced view of the structure of the novel had been presented by Jerome Thale in *The Novels of George Eliot* (New York: Columbia University Press, 1959), and Peter Coveney in his Introduction to the Penguin edition has made a convincing case for the unity of *Felix Holt* in terms of Eliot's poetic and political vision.

5   See, e.g. W. J. Harvey, *The Art of George Eliot* (London: Chatto & Windus, 1961), pp. 131–4.
6   David Craig, 'Fiction and the Rising Industrial Classes', *Essays in Criticism*, 17 (1967), 64–75.
7   For an account of the assertion of 'Gothic liberties', see Samuel Kliger, *The Goths in England: A Study in Seventeenth and Eighteenth-Century Thought* (Cambridge, Mass.: Harvard University Press, 1952).
8   Kettle, op. cit., 107.
9   V. S. Pritchett, *The Living Novel* (New York: Reynal & Hitchcock, 1947), p. 90.
10 Kettle, op. cit., pp. 108 ff.
11 Fred C. Thomson, *'Felix Holt* and Classical Tragedy', *Nineteenth-Century Fiction*, 16 (1961), 47–58.

13 'This Petty Medium': In the Middle of *Middlemarch*

JOHN F. HULCOOP

With the proof of Part I of 'Janet's Repentance' in his possession, John Blackwood writes advising George Eliot to '*soften*' her picture of life as much as she can. 'Your sketches this time are all written in the harsher Thackerayan view of human nature.' Thackeray, he adds, is 'rather disposed to claim you as a disciple of his'.[1] Defending what Haight calls 'the artistic integrity of her realism',[2] Eliot responds: 'I may have some resemblance to Thackeray, though I am not conscious of being in any way a disciple of his, unless it constitutes discipleship to think him, as I suppose the majority of people with any intellect do, on the whole the most powerful of living novelists' (*Letters*, ii, 349). This was in 1857, almost a decade after the publication of *Vanity Fair,* and fifteen years before *Middlemarch* would be completed. Yet, though separated by nearly a quarter of a century, these novels are united by the bleakly ironic view of social life and human nature shared by their very different authors.

When the Showman of *Vanity Fair* appears 'before the curtain on the boards, and looks into the Fair, a feeling of profound melancholy comes over him'.[3] When Book Four of *Middlemarch* appeared before the public in June 1872, and was reviewed by R.H. Hutton, George Eliot wrote to Blackwood 'that the Spectator considers me the most melancholy of authors' (*Letters*, v, 296). This author, says Hutton in a review entitled 'The Melancholy of *Middlemarch*', 'throws cold water with a most determined hand on the idealism, as she evidently thinks it, which interprets by faith what cannot be interpreted by sympathy and sight'.[4] Never-

theless, 'the deepest symptom of melancholy in this book is the
disposition . . . to draw the most reflective and most spiritual
characters as the least happy' (*CH*, 299). The 'height of this un-
happiness comes out in the authoress's own comments on the universe'. She sides with 'the power that wars against evil' and hopes
that 'she can do something on that side':

> But she has a very poor hope of the issue. She sees evil, and sees
> it not seldom unmixed with good in the hearts around her. . . .
> She sees narrowness so oppressive to her that she is constantly
> laughing a scornful laugh over it, and despairing of any better
> euthanasia for it than its extinction. . . . She is a melancholy
> teacher, — melancholy because sceptical; and her melancholy
> scepticism is too apt to degenerate into scorn (*CH*, 301–2).

Eliot's morbid anatomy of 'the unreformed provincial mind'[5]
and of 'the pinched narrowness of provincial life at that time' (58:
431) affords overwhelming evidence to support Hutton's interpretation. *Middlemarch*, as Leslie Stephen observes, is George Eliot's
answer to the question, 'What on the whole is your judgment of
commonplace English life?' But her answer, as Stephen quickly
indicates, makes it clear that '"provincialism" is not really confined to the provinces'.[6] Hence the irony of Rosamond's assuming
that 'Lydgate would be persuaded to leave Middlemarch and settle in London, which was "so different from a provincial town"'
(75: 552). The *Middlemarch* narrator confirms the fact that 'the
intolerable narrowness and purblind conscience of the society'
surrounding Dorothea and Lydgate is not confined to 'the unfriendly mediums of Tipton and Freshitt' (4: 27–8), to what Will
calls the 'dreadful imprisonment' of Lowick (39: 287), or to 'the
prosaic neighbourhood of Middlemarch' itself (34: 236), that
'pretty bit of midland landscape' inhabited by 'midland-bred
souls' (12: 77) who are, as Rosamond states with awful, unselfcon-
scious irony, 'very tuneless' and 'very stupid' (16: 118, 120). The
narrator leaves no doubt that, just as Brooke's 'standing for Middlemarch' (6: 42) is both a political and figurative representation,
so Middlemarch — a paradoxical place-name — stands for both a
fictitious town in the midlands and that ever-expanding section of
human society whose marches are contiguous, on the one hand,
with the aristocracy, on the other, with the proletariat.

Middlemarch, like Hayslope and Stoniton in *Adam Bede*, resonates with the harmonics of a Bunyanesque allegory, whereas the title of *Vanity Fair* sounds its tonic. Though apt in an age in which society can be divided into two classes — the literate (aristocrat and cleric) and illiterate (aristocrat and peasant) — allegory seems out of place in the middle-class or bourgeois world because, as Culler explains, it 'stresses the difference between levels, [and] flaunts the gap we must leap to produce meaning'. Allegory is 'the mode which recognizes the impossibility of fusing the empirical and the eternal and thus demystifies the symbolic relation [between "signifier" and "signified"] by stressing the separateness of the two levels, the impossibility of bringing them together'.[7] Though the 'levels' in Culler's discussion are of meaning and interpretation, they clearly have social and political correspondents since all literary forms are, in some respect, cultural models. Thackeray's novel, like Thackeray himself, tends more toward the extremes of satire and caricature than George Eliot's *Middlemarch*; Thackeray wants to stress the differences, flaunt the gap between class levels, and his title fires the first salvo in a savage attack on English society displayed from the royal family right down to the wretched Raggles and the 'pedlars, punters, tumblers, students, and all' (*VF*, 631) with whom Becky associates in Pumpernickel. The latter is another characteristic instance of Thackeray's use of place-names since Pumpernickel occasions some of his coarsest and most unbolted satire (see 'pumpernickel', *OED*). His juxtaposition of extremes — 'Satire and Sentiment' (*VF*, 158), the romantic with the low mimetic and ironic fictional modes — is a major rhetorical strategy in *Vanity Fair*.

In *Middlemarch*, however, Eliot avoids social, modal and rhetorical extremes and focuses on the middle or medium. Sir James Chettam, a member of the minor aristocracy,[8] is as high as she reaches on the social scale. Looking down, she drops in on the Dagleys, who illustrate 'the depression of agricultural interest' and 'the sad lack of farming capital, as seen constantly in the newspapers of that time' (39: 289). Though poor, the Dagleys are still tenant farmers, below the landed gentry and yeomanry but above the ploughman and farm-labourer:[9] in other words, the middle of their particular class. Two relatively 'low' scenes are set in the Tankard, a pub in Slaughter Lane run by Mrs Dollop, the 'spirited' landlady 'accustomed to dominate her company' (71: 529, 531). But the company, which acts as a 'chorus', consists of a dyer, a glazier, and a shoemaker, all artisans and therefore in the middle of their class; in addition, a barber who feels himself above the clientele at Dollop's (71: 530), and a clerk. These characters are lower middle class, and quite different from working-class characters like Stephen Blackpool, John Barton, and Joe Scott.

The focus in *Middlemarch* is clearly, even relentlessly, on that vast and, in the 1830s, increasingly difficult-to-define social area loosely demarcated by the social ranks above and below, and inhabited by the middle class (middlemarchers), those 'burghers of a midland town and surrounding parishes in which "the middle-aged fellows carry the day"' (10: 66); and in which 'a multitude of middle-aged men' who 'once meant to shape their own deeds and alter the world a little' actually 'go about their vocations in a daily course determined for them in much the same way as the tie of their cravats' (15: 107). This is that appallingly 'petty medium of Middlemarch' which Lydgate so quickly discovers is too strong for him to withstand in the Tyke affair (18: 139), as unfriendly as 'the unfriendly mediums of Tipton and Freshitt', and about as easy to breathe or move in freely as it is in the 'dim and clogging medium' of Casaubon's mind, so fittingly identified with Lowick.

This is the hugely depressing and soul-destroying medium in which George Eliot's characters exist, or struggle to exist, 'hemmed in by a social life which seemed nothing but a labyrinth of petty courses, a walled-in maze of small paths that led nowhither' (3: 21). It is also the hugely impressive medium through which George Eliot calls her characters into existence since the 'petty medium of Middlemarch', that 'prosaic neighbourhood', is identified metonymically with the author's own medium, namely, prose itself, and contrasted in a variety of ways with poetry, with the *epos* that St 'Theresa's passionate, ideal nature' demanded for its fulfilment and expression (Prelude: 3); and with the 'many-volumed romances of chivalry' recording the ideals of an earlier age, like the castles in the famous first chapter of Book Four in *The Mill on the Floss*, 'raised by an earth-born race, who had inherited from their mighty parent a sublime instinct for form'.[10] These castles 'thrill' the narrator with 'a sense of poetry' and she contrasts them with the 'dismal remnants of commonplace houses ... the sign of a sordid life' (*MF*: 237–8). 'It is a sordid life ... this of the Tullivers and Dodsons' — and neither family would be out of place in Middlemarch — 'irradiated by no sublime principles, no romantic visions, no active, self-renouncing faith ...

surely the most prosaic form of human life' (*MF*: 238).

Beginning Chapter 15 of *Middlemarch*, the narrator marches 'our living pettiness' under the 'huge legs' of that colossus, Henry Fielding, the 'great historian, as he insisted on calling himself' (104), who confidently claimed for his second novel the Augustan title of 'a comic epic poem in prose'. She proceeds to analyse Lydgate's ambitions and describes him as a man who 'dream[s] of himself as a discoverer' (15: 108). She also reveals his grandly romantic past, his affair with the French actress, Laure, to whom he displays 'the chivalrous kindness which helped to make him morally lovable' (15: 112). Three chapters later he has been overwhelmed by the 'petty medium of Middlemarch', just as he will finally succumb to carrying 'the burthen of [Rosamond's] life upon his arms', accepting 'his narrowed lot with sad recognition' (81: 586), looking passively at his future self, and seeing his own figure 'led with dull consent into insipid misdoing and shabby achievement' (79: 574). He has, much earlier, imagined 'how two creatures who loved each other, and had a stock of thoughts in common, might laugh' over their fall in fortunes; but he has also acknowledged that 'the glimpse of that poetry seemed as far off from him as the carelessness of the golden age' (69: 514). His poetic aspirations, chivalric dreams of discovery, philanthropic desires 'to do . . . great work for the world' (15: 110) are diverted through the narrow channel of mediocre, middle-class provincial life into insipid Middlemarch misdoings, and his final shabby achievement is prosaic indeed: he writes 'a treatise on Gout, a disease which has a good deal of wealth on its side' (Finale: 610). That Lydgate should consent to be led by a woman who embodies the pettiness of the Middlemarch medium, who is preoccupied with 'the petty solicitudes of middle-class gentility' (58: 424), to whom the doctor ('foreign to Middlemarch') offers 'vistas of that middle-class heaven, rank' and who thinks 'it would be especially delightful to enslave a man of talent' (12: 88),[11] is further evidence of Eliot's melancholy view of social life and human nature.

Her view of what happens to Dorothea and Will, Mary and Fred is equally uncompromising in its bleakness, the only difference being that this quartet is more or less indigenous to Middlemarch.[12] Lydgate begins as an outsider which is what makes his story so painful; the reader is forced to watch him ingested by the 'petty medium': 'Middlemarch . . . counted on swallowing Lydgate and assimilating him very comfortably' (15: 114) — which it does, to the reader's discomfort. The irony implicit in Dorothea's character and situation is brilliantly revealed in a single sentence in the opening paragraph of the novel: 'her mind was theoretic, and yearned by its nature after some lofty conception of the world which might frankly include the parish of Tipton and her own rule of conduct there; she was enamoured of intensity and greatness' (1: 6). The discrepant truth is made explicit seventy-five chapters later when she promises to clear Lydgate's name of the sinister implications of his involvement with Bulstrode. 'Dorothea's voice, as she made this childlike picture of what she would do, might have been almost taken as a proof that she could do it *effectively*' (76: 559), italics mine). The really damning comment follows almost immediately and ironically in parenthesis: '(Of lower experience such as plays a great part in the world, poor Mrs. Casaubon had a very blurred, short-sighted knowledge, little helped by her imagination)'. Her relationships with both Casaubon and Ladislaw are a direct consequence of her social myopia and her middle-class imagination which, less selfish than Rosamond's, inclines nevertheless towards naive and sentimental romanticism.

Just as Lydgate relinquishes his sense of the poetry of life, succumbs to the 'petty medium' and writes a treatise on gout, so Dorothea is disillusioned by her short-sighted idealisation of the man she supposes to hold the Key to All Mythologies and, when she remarries, chooses Ladislaw, a man who offers her a dazzling definition of poetry early in the novel (22: 166), who feels 'his literary refinements were usually beyond the limits of Middlemarch perception' (46: 337), but who stays in Middlemarch and writes political pieces in the *Pioneer*, directed by the bourgeois-minded Brooke: 'Ladislaw had now accepted his bit of work, though it was not that indeterminate loftiest thing which he had once dreamed of as alone worthy of continuous effort'. His ambition settles to 'making the "Pioneer" celebrated as far as Brassing (never mind the smallness of the area. . .)' (46: 338). Even though Will finally gets returned to Parliament 'by a constituency that pays his expenses', Chettam and the rest of Middlemarch regard 'Dorothea's second marriage as a mistake':

> she was spoken of to a younger generation as a fine girl who married a sickly clergyman, old enough to be her father, and in little more than a year after his death gave up her estate to

marry his cousin — young enough to have been his son, with no property, and not well-born. Those who had not seen anything of Dorothea usually observed that she could not have been 'a nice woman', else she would not have married either the one or the other (Finale: 612).

Though these comments belong to the ironic narrator, Dorothea herself admits to Celia that she 'might be a wiser person' and 'might have done something better, if [she] had been better' (84: 601). But she is not. And neither is Ladislaw, 'the dangerous young sprig . . . with his opera songs' (38: 278), over whom critical debate has raged long and hard. My reading of *Middlemarch* convinces me that we cannot and must not confuse the narrator's view of Will with that of Dorothea who is not only socially and psychologically myopic (like the rest of her class) but for whom a 'life . . . not filled with emotion' is impossible (Finale: 610).

Marriage itself is given the narrator's ironic eye in that most desolate of all Finales. Marriage, she states, 'which has been the bourne of so many narratives, is still a great beginning, as it was to Adam and Eve' (607–8). But, since '[e]very limit is a beginning as well as an ending', a great beginning in matrimony is also a great limit — which logic is endorsed by the adverb-modifier alluding to Adam and Eve. Returning from her honeymoon, spent in the 'sordid present' of Rome rather than in Eden (20: 143), Dorothea is forced to acknowledge that marriage is 'a moral imprisonment' (28: 189). And in Chapter 42, which is in every important sense the very middle of *Middlemarch*, Dorothea, confronted with 'the petty anxieties of [Casaubon's] self-assertion' and suffering the 'unresponsive hardness' he inflicts on her (311: 12), 'resolve[s] submission', shutting 'her best soul in prison, paying it only hidden visits, that she might be petty enough to please him' (313). And even Rosamond's 'discontent in her marriage' is due, in the narrator's ever-ironic view, 'to the conditions of marriage itself, to its demand for self-suppression and tolerance' (75: 552). Caleb Garth sums up what seems to be the novel's prevailing attitude toward the central and sustaining institution of middle-class life when he declares that 'Marriage is a taming thing' (68: 506).

He is thinking of Fred Vincy and how, if he were married to Mary, he would need less of Mr Garth's 'bit and bridle'. Though Fred's 'poetic' vision of the future, like his sister's, is one of 'the

middle-class heaven' — rank and the privilege that comes with
property and wealth — Mary Garth's view of the world, and her
future place in it, is, like her creator's, more prosaic than that of
any other character. Nevertheless, Mary is subjected to the same
painful treatment as everyone else in the discomposing Finale.
Certainly we are told (in a phrase that associates them with frog-
faced Joshua Rigg, another owner of Stone Court, whose aim is to
marry a girl with undeniable 'connections in a solid middle-class
way' [4: 302]), that Fred and Mary achieve 'a solid mutual happiness' (Finale: 608); but ironic overtones are undeniable in the
once so independent Mary's having three boys, particularly when
the narrator comments on the fact in a double negative that in-
stantly conjures a subliminal image of Lady Macbeth: 'Mary was
not discontented that she brought forth men children only' (608).
The solidity of their achievement, though not shabby like Lydgate's, is undeniably prosaic. Fred produces a work on the 'Cultivation of Green Crops and the Economy of Cattle-Feeding',
authorship of which is ascribed to Mary, since Middlemarch 'had
never expected Fred Vincy to write on turnips and mangel-wur-
zel'. Doubly ironic is the sexist prejudice which ascribes Mary's
book, 'Stories of Great Men Taken from Plutarch', to Fred because 'he had been to the University "where the ancients were
studied"'.... In this way it was made clear that Middlemarch
had never been deceived, and that there was no need to praise
anybody for writing a book, since it was always done by somebody
else (Finale: 608. Cf. the story of Joseph Liggins recounted by
Haight, 244).

Edmund Gosse suggests that, between 1864 and 1869, George
Eliot 'devoted herself to various experiments in verse' because 'she
realized what was her chief want as a writer of imaginative prose'
— namely, the ability to make her prose sing. 'I do not question
that she felt this lack herself, and that it was this which, subcon-
sciously, led her to make a profound study of the art of verse.'[13]
Whether or not Gosse's hypothesis is correct, Eliot clearly gave
considerable thought to the different technical demands of verse
and prose and, more importantly, to the symbolic value of these
two modes of literary discourse. In a note written 'some time between the appearance of 'Middlemarch'' and that of "Theoph-
rastus Such"' (according to C.L. Lewes), Eliot asked herself 'Is
the time we live in prosaic?' She answers herself as follows: 'That
depends: it must certainly be prosaic to one whose mind takes a

prosaic stand in contemplating it'. 'But it is precisely the most poetic minds that most groan over the vulgarity of the present, its degenerate sensibility to beauty, eagerness for materialistic explanation, noisy triviality.'[14]

Too many studies of the language of *Middlemarch* have been published to allow enumeration here. And though Robert Kiely, in his excellent article on 'The Limits of Dialogue in *Middlemarch*', begins by emphasising Eliot's belief in 'the psychological and social power of language' (a belief derived in part from her study of Feuerbach),[15] he does not make the direct connection I am suggesting: namely, that Eliot's artistic medium, prose, becomes in the course of the novel, a major metonymy for 'the prosaic neighbourhood' in which these fictitious events occur, and for the 'petty medium of Middlemarch' in and through which these characters have real and imagined existence. I have not implied, nor do I wish to, that Eliot regarded prose as somehow inferior to poetry: obviously, prose has its own poetry which distinguishes it from the effects of verse. I am simply taking seriously her statement that the 'historical conditions of society may be compared with those of language' (*Essays*, 287), and suggesting that she uses the word *medium* to mean both the agency by which she communicates with her reader *and* the class and quality of life as it was lived in the bourgeois world of Middlemarch at the time of the First Reform Bill, and, for reasons already suggested, in the bourgeois world beyond the provinces, in her own time, and indeed in ours.

Prose, says Virginia Woolf, 'has taken all the dirty work on to her shoulders', and become a 'beast-of-burden', compelled by novelists to carry 'loads of details, bushels of facts': it has 'answered letters, paid bills, written articles, made speeches, served the needs of businessmen, shopkeepers, lawyers, soldiers, peasants'.[16] Certainly, as a modifier, 'prosaic' is the most common, because accurate, metaphor for commonplace life in a bourgeois world well represented by Mr Brooke and Mrs Cadwallader who, not technically burghers, have nevertheless been fatally infected by the values and attitudes of what Eliot elsewhere identifies as the 'Fourth Estate'. They distrust extremes and cling to the middle way, to the median or medium and, consequently, to the mediocre—which, be it understood, means 'Of middling quality; neither bad nor good; indifferent' (*OED*). From childhood to young womanhood, Eliot knew this world inside out; after establishing her relationship with Lewes she also knew it from the outside in. 'Hers was the middle position of conservative-liberalism; it is not a position easy to sustain.'[17] And what Basil Willey says as he tries to place Eliot in terms of her religious affiliations seems equally true of her position in terms of social and political attitudes — an assertion supported by the famous, or infamous, 'Address to Working Men', just a year before she makes the first mention of *Middlemarch* (*Letters*, v, 16). She moves, as Raymond Williams rightly observes, 'more powerfully than any of our novelists in that profoundly difficult transitional world', that 'period *between* cultures, in which the old confidence of individual liberation has gone and the new commitment to social liberation has not yet been made'.[18] *Middlemarch*, Williams states, 'stands *between*' the radicalism of *Felix Holt*, which 'ends by confirming the sense of deadlock', and the faith of *Daniel Deronda*, a faith in 'an effective emigration — not the functional emigration of earlier nineteenth-century novels ... the guiding of loved characters to a simpler and happier land, but a spiritual emigration, a deeply felt, deeply desired transcendence' (Williams, p. 89, italics mine).

The melancholy that Hutton, Leslie Stephen, and many subsequent readers feel to be a potent part of their response to *Middlemarch* derives, I believe, from the fact that no such emigration or transcendence occurs at the end of the novel. The reader, like the characters, is left at the end in the middle of Middlemarch, which accounts for what I have called that most desolate of all Finales. What gives pain to the reader is Eliot's painstaking exploration of life 'in the middle' or life 'in between' — life in that petty medium for which her own expansive, all-absorbing prose and 'provincial' England become the major metaphors. Furthermore, like Scott, for whom she felt almost unqualified admiration, Eliot selects as her central figure, or figures, 'a more or less mediocre, average English gentleman' in Lydgate, and a more or less mediocre, average English gentlewoman in Dorothea.[19] In Lukács' view, Scott's 'mediocre heroes ... are unsurpassed in their portrayal of the decent and attractive as well as narrow-minded features of the English middle-class"' (Lukács, 35); but Eliot's mediocre heroes and heroines come a very close second. Lukács suggests that, in building 'his novels round a "middling", merely correct and never heroic "hero,"' Scott proves his 'exceptional and revolutionary epic gifts, although from a psychological-biographical point of view, no doubt his own personal, petty aristocratic-conservative prejudices did play an important part in the choice of these heroes' (Lukács, 33). Eliot's 'exceptional and revolutionary epic gifts' are similarly demonstrated in *Middlemarch*. From the first paragraph of the Prologue (with its allusions to 'epos' and 'epic life') to the penultimate paragraph of the Finale (which informs us that the 'determining acts' of Dorothea's life were 'the mixed result of young and noble impulse struggling under prosaic conditions',[20] and that 'the medium in which [Theresa's and Antigone's] ardent deeds took shape has gone forever'), Eliot draws the critic's attention to the fact that she is after something of epic proportion. Obviously, a conventional epic is, under the religious, social and political circumstances, out of the question, as is 'a comic epic poem in prose'. Comedy celebrates the secure moral basis on which society stands and expresses an optimistic view of the future, neither of which George Eliot could do.

What she achieves is, nonetheless, astounding: a bourgeois epic (the common critical term for the novel as literary form) which is, in fact, the symbol of itself. The author's prosaic medium, in which the deeds of mediocre hero and heroine take their shape and have their being, is also the petty social medium or bourgeois world which counts on swallowing not only Lydgate but also Dorothea, and assimilating them very comfortably (15: 114) — which it does. This process of swallowing and assimilating would-be individualists, as well as other classes, is described by Roland Barthes in his essay, 'The bourgeoisie as a joint-stock company'.[21] He calls it the 'ex-nominating phenomenon': 'the bourgeoisie has obliterated its name in passing from reality to representation, from economic man to mental man'. It is defined as *the social class which does not want to be named*.

This anonymity of the bourgeoisie becomes even more marked when one passes from bourgeois culture proper to its derived, vulgarized and applied forms. . . . These 'normalized' forms attract little attention, by the very fact of their extension, in which their origin is easily lost. They enjoy an intermediate position: being neither directly political nor directly ideological, they live peacefully between the action of the militants and the quarrels of the intellectuals; more or less abandoned by the former and latter, they gravitate towards the enormous mass of the undifferentiated, of the insignificant, in short, of nature (Barthes, 140).

Eliot's awareness of the beginnings of this extraordinary, exno-
minating phenomenon is quickly proved by a reading of one of
her most important reviews, 'The Natural History of German
Life', specifically in her discussion of von Riehl's conception of
the 'Fourth Estate' seen as both 'the sign and result of the decomposition which is commencing in the organic constitution of
society' (*Essays*, 294–5). Drawing its elements from all classes, the
Fourth Estate is 'only just awakening to the consciousness of its
corporate power. Its elements are derived alike from the aristocracy, the bourgeoisie, and the peasantry'. Its tendency, says
Eliot, 'is to do away with the distinctive historical character of the
other estates, and to resolve their peculiar rank and vocation into
a uniform social relation founded on an abstract conception of
society' (*Essays*, 295).

Middlemarch articulates the awakening consciousness of the
corporate power of the bourgeoisie. Miss Brooke and Mr Lydgate
are swallowed up by and absorbed into 'the enormous mass of the
undifferentiated' which is Middlemarch itself. Although, from a
psychological-biographical viewpoint, one must admit that Eliot's
conservative-liberal prejudices, her preference for the middle
position, helped to determine her choice of mediocre heroine and
hero, her 'exceptional and revolutionary epic gifts' enabled her to
see beyond personal prejudice, to identify the decomposition of
'historical society' (*Essays*, 295), and to acknowledge the melancholy inevitability of the all-absorbing, ex-nominating processes
of the bourgeois world. And what she so clearly saw, even though
she obviously suffered in the seeing, she reveals in a work whose
sheer bulk matches metaphorically the ever-expanding bourgeoisie, a work whose epic aspirations are persistently undermined by
the petty medium in which it has its existence, and by the prosaic
conditions of an imperfect social state against which it struggles.
The improperly extreme death-agonies of Dorothea and Lydgate
are muffled by the babel of Brookes, Cadwalladers, Chettams,
Farebrothers, Vincys, Bulstrodes and the rest. The not-so-silent
majority prevails. 'If we had a keen vision of all ordinary human
life, it would be like hearing the grass grow and the squirrel's
heart beat, and we should die of that roar which lies on the other
side of silence. As it is, the quickest of us walks about well wadded
with stupidity' (20: 144).

NOTES

1   *The George Eliot Letters*, ed. Gordon S. Haight, 9 vols (New Haven: Yale University Press, 1954–78), II, 344–5. Subsequent references are to *Letters*.
2   Gordon S. Haight, *George Eliot: A Biography* (Oxford: Clarendon Press, 1968), p. 234. Subsequent references are to Haight.
3   Thackeray, *Vanity Fair*, ed. Geoffrey and Kathleen Tillotson (Boston: Houghton Mifflin, 1963), p. 5. Subsequent reference is to *VF*.
4   *Spectator*, 45 (1 June 1872), 685–7. Reprinted in *George Eliot: The Literary Heritage*, ed. David Carroll (London: Routledge & Kegan Paul, 1971), p. 298. Subsequent references are to *CH*.
5   George Eliot, *Middlemarch*, ed. Gordon S. Haight (Boston: Houghton Mifflin, 1956), Ch. 61, p. 449. Subsequent references are to this edition.
6   Leslie Stephen, *George Eliot* (London: Macmillan, 1902), p. 174.
7   Jonathan Culler, *Structuralist Poetics: Structuralism, Linguistics and the Study of Literature* (London: Routledge & Kegan Paul, 1975), p. 230. Significantly, Eliot moves more overtly toward allegory as she descends the social scale, i.e. moves towards one of the social extremes. Bulstrode and Raffles are both criminals and therefore belong at the bottom of most social models.
8   The Dowager Lady Chettam would challenge this evaluation (84: 595).
9   Hiram Ford and Timothy Cooper, both farm-labourers, make a brief but significant appearance in Chapter 56 (404–9). For a concise discussion of the subtleties and complexities of the English class system see Richard Faber's *Proper Stations: Class in Victorian Fiction* (London: Faber and Faber, 1971).
10 Ed. Gordon S. Haight (Boston: Houghton Mifflin, 1961), p. 237. Subsequent references are to *MF*.
11 Lydgate 'once called her his basil plant; and when she asked for an explanation, said that basil was a plant which had flourished wonderfully on a murdered man's brains' (Finale, 610).
12 Though Will's origins lie outside the area, he is related by blood to Casaubon, and by Bulstrode's first marriage to Bulstrode. 'I would rather stay in this part of the country', Will says. 'I belong to nobody anywhere else' (37: 269).
13 *Aspects and Impressions* (New York: Charles Scribner's Sons, 1922), pp. 11–12.
14 'Leaves From a Note-Book', reprinted in *Essays of George Eliot*, ed. Thomas Pinney (London: Routledge & Kegan Paul, 1963), p. 448. The quotation from Charles Lee Lewes appears on p. 437. Subsequent references are to *Essays*.
15 In *The Worlds of Victorian Fiction, Harvard English Studies*, ed. Jerome Buckley (Cambridge, Mass.: Harvard University Press, 1975), p. 103.
16 'The Narrow Bridge of Art', in *Granite and Rainbow* (London: The Hogarth Press, 1958), pp. 17, 22.
17 Basil Willey, *Nineteenth Century Studies: Coleridge to Matthew Arnold* (London: Chatto & Windus, 1949), p. 238.
18 *The English Novel: From Dickens to Lawrence* (London: Chatto & Windus, 1970), p. 88. Italics mine. Subsequent reference is to Williams.

19   Georg Lukács, *The Historical Novel* (Harmondsworth: Penguin Books, 1969), p. 32. Subsequent references are to 'Lukács'.
20   The text here is that of the first edition, substantively different from the 1874 text. Haight notes the difference (Finale: 612, footnote 1).
21   *Mythologies*, selected and translated from the French by Annette Lavers (New York: Hill and Wang, 1977), p. 138. Subsequent reference is to 'Barthes'.

Index

167